Renewable Energy Made Simple: A Beginner's Guide to a Sustainable Future

Sebastian J. Wongv

Introduction

Welcome to this book, a comprehensive journey through the captivating realm of sustainable power sources that are reshaping the future of our planet. In this guide, we'll explore the multifaceted world of renewable energy, uncovering the mysteries behind their generation, their practical applications, and their undeniable potential to revolutionize the way we power our lives.

The journey begins with a deep dive into the world of hydrogen, as we unravel the reasons "Why we should all love hydrogen." Discover the remarkable versatility of this element, its profound impact on history, and its pivotal role in reshaping our energy landscape. From its humble origins to its potential as a game-changing fuel, hydrogen emerges as a beacon of hope in our quest for a greener future.

Stepping into the heart of "What is hydrogen?" we navigate the molecular intricacies of this element. Through lucid explanations, we demystify the science behind hydrogen, laying the foundation for an in-depth exploration of its various applications in the renewable energy domain.

As we travel through time, "Hydrogen in human history" reveals the integral role hydrogen has played in shaping civilizations. From its early uses to modern-day applications, the historical journey of hydrogen unveils its unending potential to power our lives.

Venturing deeper, we unveil the intricate processes that enable hydrogen's power. "How hydrogen is produced, processed and stored" takes us through steam reforming, gasification, and electrolysis, shedding light on the techniques that transform hydrogen into a viable energy source. We delve into methods like enzymatic hydrogen production and explore diverse hydrogen storage approaches, from pressurized storage to material-based solutions.

Practical applications come to the forefront as we delve into "Practical application and uses of hydrogen." The industrial realm becomes a canvas for hydrogen's prowess, from hydrocracking to ammonia production, hydrogenation to dehydrogenation. We journey into the realm of fuel cells and understand their five general advantages over conventional power sources.

But our exploration doesn't end with hydrogen; it's only the beginning. "Where are we now?" navigates the current landscape of renewable energy, from generating hydrogen fuel to fueling vehicles and exploring diverse power generation methods. From the promise of hydrogen fuel vehicles to the untapped potential of static generation, we grasp the present state of renewable energy adoption.

The guide further casts a spotlight on other prominent clean energy sources. "Other clean energy production methods" takes us through the captivating world of solar energy, hydro power, energy from oceans, geothermal, biomass, nuclear power, and wind power. We weigh their advantages and disadvantages, revealing how each contributes to reshaping the energy ecosystem.

Delve into the intricacies of large-scale and small-scale energy production with "Large scale energy production (for power grids)" and "Small scale energy production (for local and individual use)." Through these chapters, we explore the dynamic possibilities of integrating renewable energy into existing grids and harnessing its potential for localized empowerment.

As you journey through this book, you'll uncover the transformative potential that renewable energy sources hold for our world. From the molecular intricacies of hydrogen to the boundless potential of solar, wind, and beyond, you'll gain a holistic understanding of how these sources are shaping the future of energy. Prepare to be inspired and informed, as you embark on a voyage that promises a cleaner, greener, and more sustainable world.

Contents

| Why we should all love hydrogen

1

What is hydrogen?

The term 'Hydrogen Economy', relating to using hydrogen as the primary fuel for vehicles and power generation was reportedly first used by John Bockris during a talk given to the General Motors Technical Centre in 1970 (although the concept had been proposed back in 1923 by the British-Indian scientist J.B.S. Haldane). Bockris went on to publish the book 'Energy, the Solar Hydrogen Alternative' in 1975.

In these pages you will find out why hydrogen has the potential to replace fossil fuels, how important it has been throughout history and all of the various techniques involved in producing, storing and using it.

To start with we have to understand some basic concepts. Firstly we need to know a little bit about atoms.

Atoms are the smallest parts of ordinary matter that have the properties of a chemical element: basically everything we can see, hear, touch or smell is made up of atoms.

Atoms consist of a nucleus and one or more electrons (negatively charged particles) that rotate around the nucleus in various stable orbits. The nucleus is made of one or more protons (positively charged particles) and neutrons (neutral particles). The only exception is hydrogen, which only has one proton, all by itself. Hydrogen, therefore, is the simplest kind of atom there is. The chemical symbol for hydrogen is 'H'.

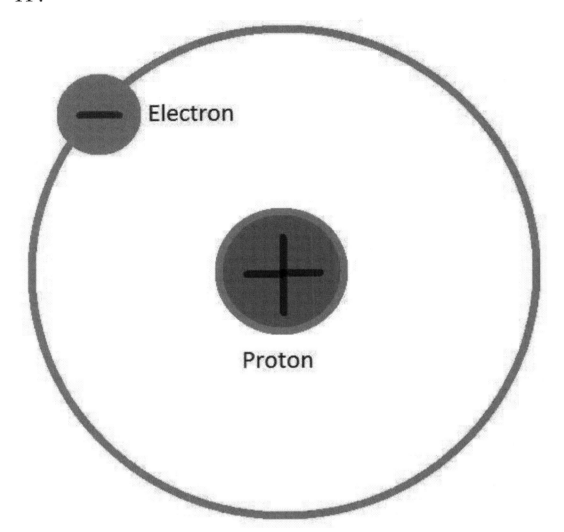

Hydrogen Atom

According to the latest scientific research, hydrogen was the first atom to form following the Big Bang that created the universe. In cosmology this is called the Recombination Epoch, during which charged electrons first became bound to protons to form electrically neutral hydrogen atoms. This happened around 378,000 years after the Big Bang.

Hydrogen is now the most abundant element in the universe, making up about 75% of normal matter by mass and 90% by number of atoms. It is the fusion of hydrogen nuclei by thermonuclear or fusion reactions that is the primary source of energy generation in stars. The scientific term for this is 'hydrogen burning', although nothing is burnt in the ordinary sense of the word. The hydrogen atoms are squashed together under increasingly immense pressures until they fuse with each-other and create the more complex atoms of the other elements, starting with helium. This releases huge amounts of energy, mostly as heat and light.

Depending on the mass and age of the star, the fusion process becomes more complex and produces all of the known elements. During the various phases of the star's life cycle, different amounts of each element are produced and released into the universe. The mass of the star partly defines the way it will develop. Some don't have enough mass to explode: our own sun is one of these. Eventually it will consume all of the hydrogen in its core. With the hydrogen fusion stopped, gravity compresses the star. This causes the temperature and pressure to increase to the point where helium begins fusing to form carbon. This releases enough energy to overcome the force of gravity and the star expands outwards to many time its original size, becoming a *red giant*.

Red giants are cooler because the matter and energy occupy a much greater volume. Helium fuses into carbon and oxygen in the core. If it has insufficient mass to generate the one billion degrees Kelvin required to fuse carbon, an inert mass of carbon and oxygen builds up in its centre. Gravity takes over again and the star shrinks until a new helium shell is formed at the core. When the fusion process starts up once more, the energy blows the outer layers of the star away to form huge clouds of dust and gas known as *planetary nebulae*. This leaves behind a core, which is known as a *white dwarf.*

White dwarf stars are thought to be the final stage in the life cycle of stars that do not have enough mass to become *neutron stars*. This includes about 97% of all the stars in our galaxy, including our sun. White dwarf stars are very dense and consist mostly of carbon and oxygen. They do not generate fusion reactions and are very hot to start with, but gradually lose this by radiation over billions of years.

Neutron stars are the ultra-dense remnants of stars that had enough mass to explode in what is called a *super nova*. There are two types of supernova. A Type 1 supernova happens when a star accumulates matter from another nearby star until a runaway nuclear reaction ignites, causing a massive explosion. A Type 2 follows the same process as other stars until the hydrogen and helium are depleted. Because of it's larger mass it has enough pressure to fuse carbon. Gradually the heavier elements are formed and build up in layers, with the heaviest elements towards the centre. Once it reaches a certain mass the star begins to implode. This makes the core become hotter and denser until the pressure in the core is so high that the implosion bounces off and ejects the surrounding stellar material into space.

So, all of the elements are formed in stars, and the process starts with hydrogen. The next thing that happens is that the atoms are attracted to each other and are able to bond together to form chains, which are called molecules. These can be composed of one element or an increasingly complex chain of combinations of elements. Hydrogen atoms are part of the molecules that make life as we know it possible. They combine with oxygen to make water (two hydrogen atoms bonded to one oxygen atom) and with carbon to create hydrocarbons, which is what all living things are made of.

The elements also have variations in their atomic structure called *isotopes*. These are atoms of an element that have the normal number of protons and electrons but a different number of neutrons. Isotopes have the same atomic number and chemical properties but with a different mass. The standard isotope of hydrogen is called *protium*. There are two other isotopes of hydrogen that you need to know about.

Deuterium (chemical symbol ^{2}H), also known as 'heavy hydrogen,' has a neutron as well as a proton. Deuterium is about twice as heavy as protium.

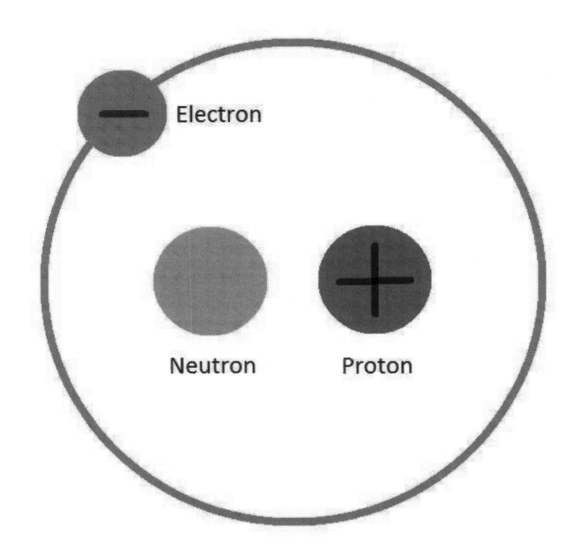

Deuterium Atom

There are an average of 26 deuterium atoms for everyone million hydrogen atoms. Water made from deuterium and oxygen is called heavy water (deuterium oxide, chemical symbol ^2H2O). It has different nuclear, physical and chemical properties compared to H2O and is used as a reaction moderator and coolant in nuclear reactors because it absorbs less neutrons than normal water, which means that natural uranium can be used for the nuclear reaction instead of enriched uranium. Deuterium is used as a non-radioactive label in chemical experiments and has other uses in scientific experiments and studies, including techniques to produce nuclear fusion.

The other hydrogen variant is *tritium* (^{3}H). This atom contains two neutrons in addition to the proton, and is radioactive.

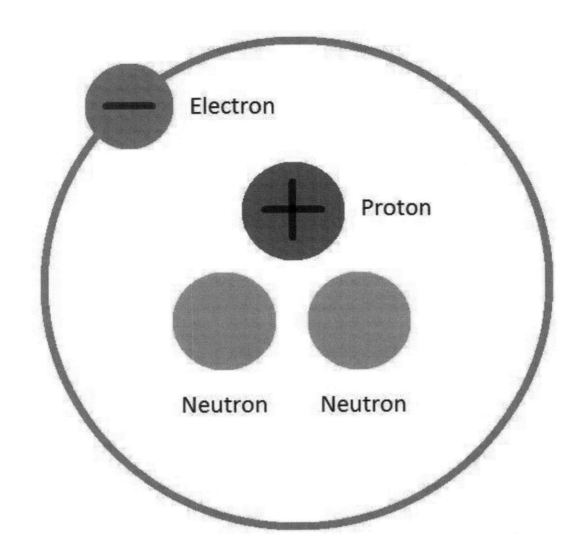

Tritium Atom

Tritium is used to make luminous paint because the electrons released by radioactive decay react with phosphors to make them glow (replacing radium which has been banned because it can cause bone cancer). It is also used in self illuminating lights found in wristwatches, dials, compasses and sights for weapons. Other uses include nuclear fusion and fission experiments (with deuterium) and as a radioactive tracer in chemical and biological experiments.

2 Hydrogen in human history

As our modern civilisation gradually emerged from the Dark Ages and became more cohesive and structured, so did the development of science and the modern scientific methodology. The modern scientific method involves making observations, formulating hypotheses, testing and experimenting, gathering data and developing theories. The results of all this have to be consistent and repeatable so that others can produce the same predicted results.

The modern scientific method began to really take shape and become universally accepted during the 17th century, when there was a lot of interest in and study of the Greek philosopher Aristotle's legacy from the 4th century BC.

As with all human development, there are lots of individual contributions along the way and then one person (or a specific group of people) suddenly puts all these things together to create something new, or build a solid platform that enables others to develop things further and faster.

Advances in technology and knowledge complement each other, and technical innovations bring about new discoveries that breed further discoveries and innovations whilst increasing our knowledge and understanding of nature.

The 17th century is often referred to as the 'Age of Reason' and is considered as the successor to the Renaissance and predecessor to the Age of Enlightenment. Work done in many fields, including philosophy, opened the path for more decisive steps towards modern science which took place during the 18th century, known as 'The Age of Enlightenment'. During the 19th century, the importance of science was recognised further and it became a proper profession with more institutions being established. This is a process that continues to this day.

17th Century – The Age of Reason

Towards the end of the 16th Century, improvements in the manufacture of optics and lenses enabled the invention of the microscope (1595), followed by the telescope in 1608. Francis Bacon postulated the basics of the modern scientific method. His work entitled 'Novum Organum Scientarium' (New instrument of science) was published in 1620.

In 1625, the Flemish chemist, physiologist and physician Jan Baptist van Helmont provided the first description of what we now call hydrogen. He is credited with introducing the word 'gas' (this is either from the Greek word for chaos or the word ghast or gheist, meaning ghost or spirit – no-one can prove it either way). Van Helmont is also considered to be the founder of 'Pneumatic Chemistry', which began as a study of the physical properties of gases and how they relate to chemical reactions. This led to improvements in laboratory techniques and a greater understanding of the Earth's atmosphere. Later on it helped establish Atomic theory, which in turn led to a greater understanding of atoms and molecules and how to measure their mass.

A key figure in the development of the scientific method was Rene Descartes, a French philosopher, mathematician and scientist. His highly influential works 'Discourse in Method' and 'La Geometrie' were published in 1637. In 1660 the Royal Society was founded in London and quickly became the UK and Commonwealth's Academy of Science.

Largely regarded as the first modern chemist, Robert Boyle published what is now known as 'Boyle's Law' in 1662. This describes how the pressure of gas tends to increase as the volume decreases. He was a founder member of The Royal Society and was elected as a Fellow of The Royal Society (FRS) in 1663. In 1670 he produced hydrogen by reacting metals with acids and published 'New Experiments Touching the Relation between Flame and Air' in 1672.

18th Century – The Age of Enlightenment

Experimentation and discovery continued apace across all fields of science and in 1766 Henry Cavendish was the first to recognise hydrogen gas as a distinct or 'discrete' substance. He called it 'Flammable Air'. In 1781 Cavendish discovered that hydrogen gas produces water when burnt, and is usually given credit for its discovery as an element.

The influential French chemist Antoine Lavoisier gave the element the name Hydrogen (from the Greek words hydro (water) and genes (creator) when he and the French scholar Laplace reproduced Cavendish's findings in 1783.

Also in 1783, the French inventor and scientist Jacques Charles, having studied the work of Robert Boyle and his contemporaries, worked in conjunction with the Robert brothers to launch the first unmanned hydrogen balloon. The experiment was a resounding success and enabled them to quickly launch the first manned flight, which lasted for over two hours and reached a height of about 550 meters (1,800 feet). More flights followed and ballooning quickly gained mass popularity. This led to increased research into ways of producing, manufacturing and storing hydrogen. It is also reflected in various articles and artwork speculating on the future, and early science fiction stories, including some of Jules Verne's writings.

19th Century

The next really important advance in science was the discovery and study of electricity. Alessandro Volta published his experiments in 1800. He wrote to the London Royal Society describing the technique for producing electric current using his device the Voltaic Pile, which was the first electrical battery that could produce a continuous electrical current to a circuit. In the same year it was used to discover how to perform electrolysis of water, in which an electric current passed through water splits it into its component gases of hydrogen and oxygen. Over the next decade the Cornish scientist and chemist Humphry Davy used the Voltaic Pile to discover and isolate the chemical elements sodium, potassium, calcium, boron, barium, strontium and magnesium.

Then, in 1806, Francois Isaac de Rivaz built the de Rivaz engine, generally acknowledged as the world's first internal combustion engine (ICE). De Rivaz had served in the French Army and his experience with cannons led him to think about using an explosive charge to drive a piston instead of using steam pressure. His first design was a stationary single cylinder engine used to drive a pump. It was fuelled with a mixture of hydrogen and oxygen which was ignited by an electric spark in the same manner as a modern ICE. In 1807 he placed his experimental engine in a carriage and made the first ICE driven vehicle. Unfortunately few of his counterparts took his work seriously (although there were others experimenting along the same lines). The French Academy of

Sciences argued that the internal combustion engine would never rival the performance of the steam engine. (This kind of thing happened more often than you would think – most famously when Lord Kelvin (one of many sceptics) stated that 'heavier than air machines are impossible' and was proved wrong by the Wright Brothers eight years later. The famous scientist and Science Fiction author Arthur C Clarke would later say, 'When a distinguished but elderly scientist says that something is possible, he is very likely right. When a distinguished but elderly scientist says that something is impossible, he is very likely wrong.')

In 1819, hydrogen was first used in a blowpipe by Edward Daniel Clarke, an English Clergyman, naturalist, chemist, mineralogist and traveller. Blowpipes are tools that channel a concentrated jet of gas through a flame to create a very hot jet. Contemporary blowtorches and welding and cutting torches are modern developments of the blowpipe. Clarke mixed the hydrogen with oxygen which vastly increased the temperature and drove the development of the gas blowpipe as a tool. This very quickly enabled its use in exploring the characteristics of heating a much larger range of materials to high temperatures.

Limelight was discovered by using the oxy-hydrogen blowpipe to rapidly heat a cylinder containing quicklime. This creates an intense illumination that is most famous for its use as stage lighting. One of its earliest uses was for indoor stage illumination at the Covent Garden Theatre in London in 1837. It became widely used in theatres around the world until it was replaced by electric arc lights in the late 1800's.

The first references to fuel cells appeared in 1838 and 1839 in letters published in 'The London and Edinburgh Philosophical Magazine and Journal of Science'. Two letters came from Welsh physicist William Grave and a third was from the German physicist Christian Schonbein. They discussed electric current generated from hydrogen and oxygen dissolved in water. Grove later supplied a sketch of his fuel cell that used similar materials to today's phosphoric acid fuel cells.

In 1866 August Wilhelm von Hoffman, a German chemist who became the first director of The Royal College of Chemistry in London in 1845, invented the Hoffman Voltammeter, an apparatus for electrolyzing water.

Hoffman voltameter

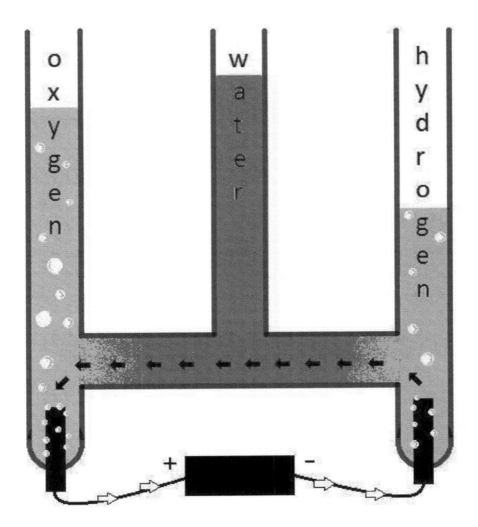

When an electric current is run through the voltammeter, gaseous oxygen is formed at the anode (positive terminal) and hydrogen is formed at the cathode (negative terminal).

Each gas displaces water and collects at the top of its tube. By comparing the amount of each gas collected from a volume of water the composition of water (H_2O) is proven, as the gas volume is 2:1 (twice as much hydrogen as oxygen). This has become a classic demonstration experiment and I have seen it both in chemistry lessons and on TV programs.

In his 1874 novel 'The Mysterious Island', Jules Verne wrote 'Water will one day be employed as fuel, in that the hydrogen and oxygen of which it is constituted will be used.'

French chemist Paul Sabatier defined what is now known as the Sabatier Process in 1897. This process is the basis of hydrogenation (a process explained in the chapter 'Practical Application and Uses of Hydrogen'). Sabatier shared the 1912 Nobel Prize in Chemistry for his pioneering work in this field.

In 1898 the Scottish chemist and physicist James Dewar liquefied hydrogen using a regenerative cooling system and invented the Vacuum Flask. Unfortunately for him, he did not patent it and so was unable to prevent the company Thermos from using his designs, and did not profit from its widespread use. He next experimented with a high powered hydrogen jet and found that extremely low temperatures could be achieved by the resulting Joule-Thomson effect (very basically the heating or cooling of gas during expansion but far too technical to explain further here). The success of these experiments enabled him to have a large regenerative cooling machine at the Royal Institution and in 1899 he collected solid hydrogen for the first time by reducing its temperature to -259.16 °C (14.01 °K).

20th Century

Airships

The 20th century started with the launch of the first hydrogen filled airship by Count Ferdinand Von Zeppelin, a former general in the German army. On retiring from the army he followed up his interest in the emerging flight technology of balloons and founded the Zeppelin Airship company. The Zeppelin LZ1 was the first successful rigid airship. It did not have enough of an impact to attract investment from the government but, with the support of the King of Wurttemburg (whom he had served as an adjutant during his army career) and a contribution from Prussia, Zeppelin was able to continue developing airships. The LZ2 made only one flight due to a series of mishaps and technical problems. In 1906 the LZ3 made two successful flights and in 1907 flew at a speed of 36 mile per hour. This achievement caught the attention of the Reichstag and increased the growing public interest in airships. A larger model, the LZ4, was destroyed by fire after breaking free of its moorings during a storm. The LZ3 was revamped and, with the Kaiser's brother as a VIP passenger, flew non-stop for five hours and fifty-five minutes on the 27th of October 1908. On the 7th of November it flew a distance of 80 km (50 miles) and on the 10th of November Zeppelin gave a short demonstration flight to the Kaiser and was awarded the Order of The Black Eagle. Zeppelins were built for the army and the company made a decision to capitalize on public enthusiasm by establishing a passenger carrying business. By 1914 the German Aviation Association had transported 37,250 people on over 1,600 flights without any incidents and the Zeppelin revolution began creating the age of air transportation.

On the 2nd of July 1919, the British made airship R34, which was the length of two football fields, left East Fortune in Scotland and completed the first transatlantic airship flight when it arrived in Mineola, New York, four and a half days later. The R34 was refuelled and turned around for the return flight, which left on the 10th of July and took seventy-five hours to fly to Norwich, England

The Zeppelin LZ129 Hindenberg was destroyed by fire in 1937. News of the tragedy rapidly spread around the world thanks to the now famous newsreel coverage and this rapidly brought about the demise of the airship as a commercial transport.

Early 20th Century

The German chemist Wilhelm Norman introduced the process for the hydrogenation of fats in 1901. This converts liquid vegetable oils into solid or semi-solid fats, such as those present in margarine. These fats are cheaper to produce than animal fats and were quickly picked up by food manufacturers, especially for baking, and were found to improve the shelf life of the product (this is explained in more detail in the chapter Practical Applications and Uses of Hydrogen).

In 1903 the British engineer Howard Lane invented the Lane Hydrogen Producer. The first commercial version was commissioned a year later and by 1913 twenty-four million square meters (850,000,000 cubic feet) of hydrogen was being produced annually, a proportion of which was used in airships. The process continued to be used until the 1920's when it was superseded by cheaper methods.

During the early part of the Twentieth Century there was a lot of research being carried out investigating the spectrums of gases, beginning with hydrogen. This research led to major advances in physics and the development of Quantum Mechanics.

Throughout the 1920's and 30's, new methods of producing hydrogen and using it for commercial purposes were developed. These methods include steam reforming and hydrocracking, which are explained in more detail later on in this book.

Having studied the explosive reaction of hydrogen and oxygen, the English physicist Cyril Norman Hinshelwood first described the chain reaction phenomena in 1926.

In 1930 the German engineer Rudolf Erren patented the Erren engine in the UK. It was described as relating to the use of a mixture of hydrogen and oxygen as a fuel for internal combustion engines. The U.S. patent was registered in 1939.

The Heinkel HeS1 hydrogen fuelled centrifugal jet engine was tested in 1937 and is recognized as the first working jet engine. In the same year, the first hydrogen cooled turbo generator went into service in Dayton, Ohio, U.S.A. Today this method for cooling steam turbines is the most common type in its field.

The Rhine-Ruhr pipeline, completed in 1938, was the first hydrogen pipeline (used to transport hydrogen from the point of production to the point of demand). It runs for 150 miles (240 km) and is still in use today.

Liquid hydrogen was tested as a rocket fuel at Ohio State University in 1943.

Nuclear Weapons

The first nuclear weapon to be developed was a fission bomb, more commonly known as the atomic or A-bomb. The fission process uses heavy radioactive materials (most commonly uranium or plutonium isotopes) because the unstable atoms decay and emit neutrons that strike other atoms, causing them to split apart. This releases more neutrons and the result is a release of energy. Under controlled conditions, this method of releasing energy is what powers a nuclear reactor.

Fission bombs use conventional explosives to force the radioactive material into a tight, extremely dense ball until it reaches critical mass, which is when the fission process starts. The core heats up exponentially until it reaches supercritical mass. When this happens it triggers a chain reaction that instantaneously releases energy equivalent to tens of thousands of tons of TNT.

The first test detonation of a fission bomb was made by the Allies in Alamogordo, New Mexico on 16th July 1945. Codenamed Trinity, it marked the successful conclusion of the Manhattan project, which was the Allies' nuclear weapon development project. Three weeks later, on 6th August 1945, a uranium fission bomb was detonated over the Japanese city of Hiroshima and three days after that a plutonium device was dropped on Nagasaki. The unprecedented destructive capacity of these two bombings and the Soviet Union's declaration of war with Japan on 8th August brought about the announcement of Japan's surrender to the Allies on 15th August. This was oficially ratified when the Japanese government signed the instrument of surrender on 2nd September, effectively ending World War II.

Although they definitely speeded up the surrender of Japan and the cessation of hostilities, the justification for the atomic detonations in Hiroshima and Nagasaki is still heavily debated.

A second type of nuclear weapon was subsequently developed. Using fusion instead of fission, these are referred to as hydrogen or H-bombs. The process involves using a fission bomb as a trigger to heat a charge consisting of the isotopes of hydrogen to a temperature of millions of degrees. The hydrogen isotopes fuse into helium that sets off a chain reaction and explosion many times larger than a fission bomb can achieve – in the order of megatons of TNT.

Ivy Mike, the code name for the first hydrogen bomb, was tested in 1952 but was quickly surpassed by a non-cryogenic (dry fuel) hydrogen bomb codenamed Shrimp. Tested in

1954, Shrimp produced a much more powerful explosion than anticipated and caused the most significant radioactive contamination accident in U.S.A. history.

Post War

During the late 1950's, Pratt and Whitney developed their model 304 jet engine using liquid hydrogen fuel as part of the Lockheed CL-400 Suntan project, intended to create a faster successor to the U2 spy plane with increased altitude capability. The project was unsuccessful due to the infrastructure costs involved, but the plane research lead directly to the conventionally powered and highly successful SR71 Blackbird. The fuel research laid the groundwork for the use of liquid hydrogen combined with liquid oxygen as a rocket fuel. This enabled the development of ever more powerful rockets that were used for the Mercury, Gemini and Apollo projects and, in fact, all commercial and scientific rocket launches. It is still the only viable rocket propellant.

The RL-10 liquid hydrogen/oxygen fuelled rocket engine made its first successful flight in 1961, and the first commercial use of hydrogen fuel cells was in project Gemini, the spaceflight testing and proving missions that tested all of the procedures needed for the Apollo moon landings.

In 1958 the specifications for a double-axle liquid hydrogen powered semi-trailer were issued and over the next few years the first hydrogen fuel cell tractor, fork lift truck and welding machine were built and demonstrated.

The American engineering company Allis-Chambers built a 750 watt fuel cell powered one man underwater research vessel in 1964 and the first fuel cell powered golf carts a year later.

In 1966, U.S. car manufacturer General Motors introduced the Electrovan, which was the first time fuel cells were used to drive the wheels of an automobile (in this case a modified Handivan). Unfortunately it was not economical to mass produce as it used platinum, and there were a host of other problems with the prototype.

Also in 1966, it was discovered that by reducing the temperature of hydrogen to around its melting point from frozen you can produce 'Slush Hydrogen'. This is 16 to 20% more dense than liquid hydrogen and was proposed as a rocket fuel to replace liquid hydrogen in order to improve the storage capacity by volume and reduce the launch weight of the vehicle. This means you use less space (volume) to carry the amount of fuel required to achieve orbit.

The liquid hydrogen/oxygen rocket engine J2 was first used in 1967. It powered the Saturn 1B and Saturn V rockets and was designed to be shut down and re-started, the first burn shutting down after placing the vehicle in Earth orbit and then reignited for a second burn to launch the vehicle into a lunar trajectory.

In the same year the Japanese chemist Akina Fujusima was working on his Ph.D under the supervision of Professor Kanichi Honda when he discovered the phenomenon of photocatalytic water decomposition (water photolysis) by exposing a titanium dioxide electrode to strong light. This is now called the Honda-Fujusima effect and is used for photo catalysis in photo electrochemical cells (PECs). These produce electrical energy (or hydrogen) in a process similar to the electrolysis of water. It has been referred to as artificial photosynthesis and could be a way of storing solar energy as hydrogen for use as a fuel. Akina Fujusima has had a long and distinguished career and is currently President of the Tokyo University of Science.

The Hydride compressor was also demonstrated for the first time in 1967. It is a method of long term hydrogen storage for use in spacecraft and automobiles.

In 1971 the nickel-hydrogen battery was patented. This is a rechargeable battery and is used in the Hubble Space Telescope, the International Space Station and on many space probes including the Mars Global Surveyor.

The European Space Agency's first launch system Ariane 1 made its debut flight on 24th December 1979. It used HM7B liquid hydrogen rocket engines to launch their CAT-1 technological test capsule into orbit.

NASA launched the first Space Shuttle in 1981. The Shuttle main engine was a liquid hydrogen and oxygen fuel cryogenic rocket engine. The Shuttle also used alkaline fuel cells to provide electricity and the water produced was used for the crew to drink and as a coolant in heat exchangers.

In 1997 Anastasios Melis, an American biologist at USC Berkeley discovered that depriving algae of sulphur makes it switch from producing oxygen to producing hydrogen. This is covered in more detail in the chapter about hydrogen production.

21st Century

The first type IV hydrogen tanks for storing compressed hydrogen at 700 bar (1,000 psi) were demonstrated in 2001.

In 2002 the first 'Hydrail' locomotive was demonstrated in Val d'or, Quebec. It was a 3.6 tonne, 17kw hydrogen powered locomotive. The latest Hydrail advance is a 380 passenger train demonstrated by CSR Sifang co ltd in Qingdao, China in 2015.

Deep C, an autonomous underwater vehicle propelled by an electric motor powered by a hydrogen fuel cell was debuted in 2004.

The Ionic Liquid Piston Compressor was first demonstrated in 2005. Used to compress hydrogen up to 1,000 bar (1,450 psi) in hydrogen fuelling stations, it is much less complex than conventional piston compressors, has a much longer service life (as much as 10 times more) and is around 20% cheaper to run.

In 2007 fuel cells had been developed to the point where they complied with the codes and standards of their target markets and began to be sold commercially, initially as Auxiliary Power Units (APU) and backup generators.

Honda began leasing their FCX Clarity fuel cell electric vehicle in California in 2008.

By 2014 the Japanese hydrogen fuel cell micro combined heat and power (MCHP) ENE-FARM project (generating electricity for individual houses or buildings on site) had sold over 100,000 systems.

2015 saw the first commercial power to gas installation in Falkenhagen, Germany. This uses electricity to produce hydrogen, which is then stored in the natural gas grid.

London's first zero carbon hydrogen refuelling station was opened in Teddington at the beginning of May 2016. It features vehicles from Hyundai, Honda and Toyota and is the first of three stations to be opened under the HyFive project. There are currently 14 hydrogen refuelling stations open in the UK and the UK government is funding and supporting further investment.

92 new hydrogen refuelling stations were opened globally in 2016, bringing the number of refuelling stations operating to 274. It is now possible to drive a fuel cell vehicle from Norway to northern Italy. California is developing their hydrogen infrastructure faster than any other state in America and more hydrogen refuelling stations are being planned and built globally than ever before as part of a increasing push towards establishing a worldwide hydrogen economy.

3 How hydrogen is produced, processed and stored

As you know from the first chapter, hydrogen is the lightest element and any that gets released into the atmosphere quickly rises up and escapes into space. Therefore, to produce hydrogen you have find trapped hydrogen and release it.

As hydrogen bonds so easily with most elements, there is a huge amount trapped in our environment. It can be released from water by using electrolysis and from hydrocarbons in many ways, the most common of which is currently steam reforming.

So, hydrogen can be produced from diverse common resources including fossil fuels, biomass and water. The environmental impact of hydrogen production depends on the method used.

Steam reforming
This is currently by far and away the most commonly used method of producing hydrogen and accounts for 85% to 90% globally. It is sometimes also referred to as Steam Methane Reforming (SMR).

High temperature steam and a methane source (most commonly from natural gas) are combined with a catalyst (usually nickel) at high pressure. This produces hydrogen, carbon monoxide and small amounts of carbon dioxide. The carbon monoxide is then reacted with steam and a different catalyst (copper or iron) at a lower temperature in what is called a gas-shift reaction. This produces more hydrogen and carbon dioxide. The final process is called pressure-swing absorption in which impurities are removed from the gas stream leaving essentially pure hydrogen as the end product.

Steam reforming can also be used to produce hydrogen and other fuels such as methanol, propane and petrol. A major disadvantage of using this method is the amount of carbon dioxide that is produced. It is possible to use carbon capture techniques to reduce the amount of CO_2 released into the atmosphere but this increases the overall production cost and is not commonly used.

Gasification

Coal has developed a bad reputation over the last century because burning it produces a lot of particle pollution (the cause of chemical smog amongst other things) and greenhouse gases. It is, however, a complex substance that can be converted into a variety of products. Gasification is a process that produces power, liquid fuels, chemicals and hydrogen from coal and other sources including petroleum coke and a variety of biomass and waste-derived feed stocks.

This process is gaining in popularity for electricity generation but it has been used in the chemical, refining and fertiliser industries for decades because it produces a mixture of mainly hydrogen and carbon dioxide call Syngas, which is used to produce methanol, nitrogen based fertilisers and hydrogen. Even the glasslike by-product of the gasification process, called slag, can be used in roofing materials and road surfacing.

In a coal fired power plant, the coal is burned to produce heat which turns water into steam to drive a turbine. This releases a whole range of pollutants and large amounts of carbon dioxide. By comparison, the gasification process uses high pressures and temperatures which cause the coal to undergo different chemical reactions. It is sometimes referred to as 'clean coal' because it doesn't involve spewing toxins and CO2 into the atmosphere. The coal, however, still has to be mined and is not a renewable energy source. Biomass gasification produces the same results but uses renewable materials such as wood, plants and organic waste as a fuel source.

Gasification was first developed by a Scottish engineer called William Murdoch in the late 1700's. He had spent most of his career developing steam engines before turning his attention to experimenting with the production and use of gases. His house in Redruth, Cornwall was the first domestic residence to be lit by gas. Apart from the benefits of gas lighting and heating, the process for producing Syngas also generated a number of other substances that were successfully exploited by other people. Among those substances were coke, ammonia, phenol (carbolic acid) and coal tar.

Phenol is a disinfectant and was used as one of the components in the first synthetic plastic – Bakelite. Coal tar contains a number of organic chemicals, including acetylsalicylic acid, more commonly known as Aspirin. Coal tar was also used to produce the first synthetic dye (mauve).

Cities in Europe and America began using Syngas (which quickly became known as Town Gas) to light their streets and houses. Eventually it was replaced by natural gas and then electricity (generated from coal burning power generation (oh dear!)).

As concerns about pollution, climate change and power generation have increased over the last few decades, gasification has been making a comeback and is becoming more eficient all the time, to the point that it is now being touted as an important source of clean, renewable energy.

Electrolysis

This is the use of electricity to split water into hydrogen and oxygen. The reaction takes place in a unit called an Electrolyser in a similar process to that used in fuel cells. They can be small units for localised hydrogen production up to large scale central production facilities. Depending on how the electricity is produced, this can be a zero emission production method.

Electrolyser

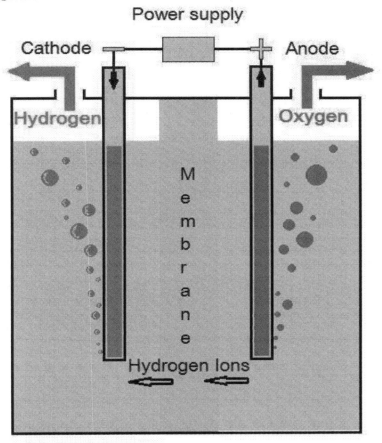

The main types of Electrolyser are as follows;
<u>Polymer Electrolyte Membrane (PEM)</u>
The electrolyte is a solid plastic based material. Oxygen is produced at the anode. The electrons pass through an external circuit and the hydrogen ions (photons) move through the PEM. At the cathode, the protons react with the

electrons to produce hydrogen gas. PEM electrolysers typically operate at between 70°C and 90°C.

Alkaline Electrolyser (AEC)

Traditionally these use a liquid alkaline solution such as sodium or potassium hydroxide as the electrolyte. New technologies are now emerging that use solid alkaline membranes. As in PEMs, oxygen is produced at the anode and hydrogen at the cathode. They typically operate in the 100°C to 150°C temperature range.

Solid Oxide Electrolyser (SOEC)

These use a solid ceramic material as the electrolyte. In this method water at the cathode combines with electrons from the external circuit to produce hydrogen gas and negatively charged oxygen ions. These pass through the ceramic membrane and react at the anode to produce oxygen gas and the electrons that flow through the external circuit to the cathode. To function properly, this process must operate at about 750°C. They can use heat produced by external sources to decrease the amount of electricity required to produce hydrogen from water.

Do try this at home

The basic method of electrolysis is extremely simple and you can do it at home. You need a nine volt battery, two paperclips and a container of water.

Unbend the paperclips (or use electrical wire). Connect one to the positive terminal of the battery and the other to the negative terminal. Then place the other ends in the container of water, as far apart as possible. You should see bubbles coming off of both wires in the water. The one with the most bubbles is producing pure hydrogen. The other is producing impure oxygen. You can test which is the hydrogen by lighting a match over the water (be careful). The hydrogen bubbles will burn whereas the impure oxygen will not. Using an electrolyte (such as salt) in the water increases the reaction but may produce small amounts of chlorine gas.

I tried this and the hydrogen gas formed quite quickly. The bubbles give a satisfying pop when lit with a match. There was very little going on at the oxygen end, but the wire oxidised quite quickly. When I used paperclips, the wire oxidised, turned brown and dissolved when left overnight. Using copper electrical wire turned the water a bluish green colour as it oxidised.

Thermochemical cycle

Adding the prefix Thermo (from the Greek thermos, meaning heat) in front of the word chemical tells us that this is a process that uses heat to produce chemical reactions. The cycle part refers to the fact that the chemicals are reused in each cycle, creating a closed loop that only consumes water and produces hydrogen and oxygen.

The process requires high temperatures (between 500°C and 2,000°C) and is still being studied and developed (there are literally hundreds of different chemical reactions that can be used) and it is hoped that providing the heat from, for instance, concentrated reflected solar energy, will provide a clean method of producing hydrogen.

Photobiological

This is a way of producing hydrogen from green algae. It is a recently developed technology mostly resulting from research by Anastasios Melis, an American biologist at the University of California, Berkeley. He is currently Professor of Plant and Microbial Biology and Editor-in-Chief of the Planta Journal, a monthly peer-reviewed scientific journal covering all areas of botany.

In 1998, following research dating back to the 1930's, Professor Melis discovered that depriving particular strains of green algae of sulphur causes them to switch from producing oxygen to producing hydrogen. Work is continuing to improve the eficiency and this is a very promising way of producing hydrogen from sunlight with low to zero carbon emissions. The algae and bacteria could be grown in water that cannot be used for drinking or agriculture, and even waste water. Bioreactors are currently being developed to maximise the potential of the process.

Photocatalytic

This is a method of producing hydrogen by artificial photosynthesis. It uses a substance called a photocatalyst and light. The latest research shows that solar water splitting using a powdered photocatalyst is an effective approach to producing hydrogen in a simple and inexpensive way.

Bacterial Biohydrogen

In a similar manner to that used in alcohol production, hydrogen can be produced by fermentation, which is a process that converts sugar to acids, gases or alcohol. Using the recently developed and ever evolving device called a bioreactor, this advanced biofuel producing technology is becoming more attractive as biohydrogen is very easy to collect from the bioreactor.

To produce hydrogen, bacteria are used with organic acids that promote high production rates to speed up the process. The most important organic acids are acetic acid, butyric acid and propionic acid. These can all be derived from any organic material, including sewage waste water and agricultural waste.

So, what is so important about these acids? Well, let's take a closer look.

Acetic acid

This is produced and excreted by certain bacteria found universally in foodstuffs, water and soil. It is also produced naturally by fruit and other vegetation as it begins to decompose and can be made synthetically using bacterial fermentation. You know it in a diluted form as vinegar, which is the oldest known application of acetic acid.

Acetic acid is also used in an extremely wide variety of applications and chemical processes. In particular, it is used to produce Vinyl Acetate Monomer (VAM), which accounts for about 45% of the global production of the acid.

VAM is used to make PVA, a type of thermoplastic used extensively in the manufacture of glues, adhesives and paints. It is also used to produce solvents, textiles, photographic film, anti-fungal creams, dyes, pigments and acidity regulator food additive E260. Current production is over eleven million tonnes per year.

Batyric Acid (BTA)

BTA is a fatty acid found in milk, butter and cheeses in varying quantities and is produced by a process called anaerobic fermentation (which is happening inside you as you read this!). Body odour and vomit smell the way they do because of the BTA in them. It was first found in butter and the name comes from the Latin word batyrum, meaning butter. Batyric acid is metabolised by the body and used by mitochondria as an energy source to power the cell (I told you it is important).

BTA is produced for industrial use by fermentation and is used to produce salts and esters (which are compounds such as fats and oils). These are used as additives for perfumes and food (including fishing baits).

Propionic Acid

This acid prohibits the growth of moulds and some bacteria and is mainly used as a preservative for animal feed and food for human consumption (E number E280). It is also used to make pesticides and pharmaceutical products. The esters of propionic acid have fruit-like odours and are used in some solvents and artificial flavourings. On the downside, it is produced by bacteria known as propionibacterium that live on human skin and is one of the principle causes of acne.

Enzymatic Hydrogen Production

This is a bit cutting edge at the moment but is showing huge potential. In experiments it has been proven that sugar glucose can be used to produce hydrogen using two enzymes; glucose dehydrogenase and hydrogenase.

Glucose is a simple sugar. It is made during photosynthesis from water and carbon dioxide using energy from sunlight. Glucose circulates in the blood of animals as blood sugar and is the most important source of energy for cellular respiration. The molecular formula for glucose is $C_6H_{12}O_6$.

Research is being carried out to develop this process and it is likely that the result will be a 'hydrogen on demand' system that produces enough hydrogen to run a fuel cell. When that happens, you should be able to generate electricity with a fuel cell using glucose as fuel.

Hydrogen Storage Methods

Hydrogen has the highest energy by mass of any fuel. This sounds wonderful but, unfortunately, at normal atmospheric pressure it has a very low density. One kilogram of hydrogen gas, which will run a current fuel cell vehicle for around 100 km, at normal atmospheric pressure and a temperature of 21° C takes up nearly 12 cubic metres. This means it has very low energy by volume which can only be improved by compression or cooling it to a liquid or slush state for storage and transportation.

A lot of research is being done at the moment into methods of storing hydrogen inside materials which can then release it as required, doing away with the problems associated with pressurisation and liquefaction.

Pressurised Storage

Currently the most common way of storing hydrogen is under pressure in large underground caverns, typically depleted oil, gas and coal fields or salt mines. From there it can either be transferred into storage tanks or gas cylinders for transport, or pumped along pressurised pipe lines in a similar fashion to natural and other gases.

At the moment a lot of hydrogen is distributed in steel cylinders at a pressure of 200 bar. (The bar is a unit of pressure defined as 100 kilopascals. One bar is approximately equal to standard atmospheric air pressure at sea level).

To further improve storage capacity, tanks and cylinders made of composite materials have been developed that are lighter than steel and allow pressures of up to 700 bar. This technology has been taken up by hydrogen fuel cell vehicle manufacturers as it means that a 125 litre tank can store 5 kg of hydrogen, which is gives a range of around 500 km for fuel cell cars.

Liquid Storage

Hydrogen starts turning into a liquid at -250° C. To put this in perspective, water freezes at 0° C, the average temperature at the North Pole is -50°C and the lowest temperature possible (absolute zero) is -273.15° C. To store hydrogen in this form requires isolated tanks capable of keeping the temperature below -250° C.

Liquid hydrogen is currently only used in high tech applications, mostly as a fuel for rockets.

Material Based Storage

This is the subject of a lot of research that is beginning to show promising results. There are two main methods, these being hydrides and LOHCs.

Hydrides

Hydrides are chemical compounds in which hydrogen is combined with other elements. Formally, a hydride is known as the negative ion of a hydrogen atom (H^-) and is also called a hydride ion. Because of this negative charge, hydrides have what is called reducing properties. This means that they donate electrons to other elements or compounds. There are three main types of hydride.

Saline (Ionic) Hydrides

Also known as ionic hydrides, these are compounds of hydrogen and active metals. Active (or alkali) metals are elements in Group One of the periodic table and include sodium, lithium and potassium. They react so strongly and quickly with other elements that they do not appear in pure form in the natural environment and require careful handling.

Saline hydrides react instantly with water to produce hydrogen gas and solution. Sodium hydride is more commonly known as caustic soda (or lye) and already has great industrial importance. Because they give off large volumes of hydrogen gas in the reaction with water, it is anticipated that they will be used as light and portable sources of hydrogen.

Metallic (Interstitial) Hydrides

These are formed when hydrogen bonds with transitional metals. These are elements that appear in Groups Two and Three of the periodic table. The better known elements in this category are iron, copper, silver and gold. They are less reactive than the alkali metals, have high density and melting points and are good conductors of electricity.

By combining one or more metals elements to form an alloy, the storage capacity and hydrogen release rate can be modified. Alloys have been traditionally made to give greater strength and resistance to corrosion. Bronze is an alloy of copper and tin and brass is 70% copper and 30% zinc. There is a lot of research being carried out in this field at the moment.

Covalent Hydrides

Consisting of compounds of hydrogen and non-metals, these are mostly liquids or gases that have low melting and boiling points, except in cases where their properties are modified by hydrogen bonding. One example of a covalent hydride is when hydrogen bonds with chlorine and forms hydrochloric acid (HCl). Others include water (H_2O), ammonia (NH_3) and hydrogen fluoride (HF). Much of the research being done is based around improving the rate of release of the hydrogen.

LOHC (Liquid Organic Hydrogen Carriers)

The storage of hydrogen in this form is seen as a break-through on the path to a hydrogen economy. An organic compound is hydrogenated using a catalyst to store the hydrogen in an easily managed liquid form and then dehydrogenated (again using a catalyst), thus releasing the hydrogen for end use.

LOHCs are similar to diesel and thus can be transported and distributed using the existing infrastructure for oil-based fuels. They also do away with the problem of hydrogen evaporation and can be stored for many months without any losses.

There are already some companies offering this service and the market will only continue to grow.

4 Practical application and uses of hydrogen

Overview

Hydrogen is already a vital part of our global economy and is set to become even more prevalent as more uses and better production and storage techniques are developed.

Because it is lighter than air, it is used as a lifting agent in weather balloons and airships. Liquid hydrogen combined with liquid oxygen is the most common form of rocket fuel. It is used in fuel cells to produce electricity and can be used as a fuel for internal combustion engines.

Currently, the most common use of hydrogen is in chemical processes and reactions. It is an important element in the process of breaking down crude oil into fuel oil, creating ammonia which is then used to make fertilizer, and as a hydrogenating agent in the manufacture of baked products and biscuits.

The chemical industry uses hydrogen to produce hydrochloric acids, methyl alcohol (for inks, varnishes and paints), hydrogen peroxide (a very important compound for medical use – most First Aid kits contain it) and as part of the process for purifying tungsten.

Welding companies use hydrogen in welding torches that can melt steel, including Atomic Hydrogen Welding (AHW).

Hydrogen fuel cells generate electricity from oxygen and hydrogen. They have a multitude of uses depending on type and are used in weather stations, spacecraft, submarines and, more recently, motor vehicles.

Most spacecraft (including the ISS and Hubble Space Telescope) use re-chargeable nickel-hydrogen batteries because of their long life (they can go through over 20,000 charge cycles).

Industrial use

Hydrogen is used in a range of industries including chemical production, metal refining, electronics manufacturing, food processing and oil refining.

Hydrocracking

This technique is an important source of diesel, jet fuel and other refined fuels.

A hydrocracking unit (called a hydrocracker) takes gas oil and cracks the heavy molecules into distillates (such as jet fuel, kerosene and diesel) and gasoline. There are two main reactions; catalytic cracking of heavy hydrocarbons into lighter unsaturated hydrocarbons, and the saturation of the newly formed hydrocarbons with hydrogen.

Hydrocarbons are organic compounds made up entirely of hydrogen and carbon. The majority of hydrocarbons found on Earth occur naturally in crude oil. The most important thing about hydrocarbons is that they like bonding together to form more complex molecules.

Unsaturated hydrocarbons are simpler hydrocarbon molecules that have the ability to absorb more hydrogen atoms. This means that they are not filled up to their limit (saturated) with hydrogen.

The hydrocracker upgrades low quality heavy oils into high quality refined fuels. Hydrogen gas is also used to regulate the temperature of the hydrocracking process.

If you want to find out a bit more detail about the hydrocracking process, follow this link.

Hydro treating is a process whereby hydrogen is used to remove impurities. It can remove up to 90% of contaminants such as nitrogen, sulphur, oxygen and metals from liquid petroleum. Without this process, catalytic converters (the emission control devices fitted to all modern Internal Combustion Engine (ICE) vehicles) would not work.

So, in order to produce the polluting fuels that we currently use in ICEs, we have to use hydrogen. I find this very disappointing as hydrogen can actually be used to fuel ICEs directly (and only emits water and trace amounts of nitrogen oxide from the exhaust), and as a fuel in fuel cells to generate electricity that powers the vehicle.

Ammonia Production

The Haber process converts atmospheric nitrogen into ammonia by a reaction with hydrogen using a metal catalyst under high pressure and temperature.

Ammonia is a compound of nitrogen and hydrogen and has the chemical formula NH_3. It is used as a building block for the synthesis of many pharmaceuticals and is also present in diluted form in many conventional cleaning products. Your kidneys secrete ammonia to neutralise excess acid. Carpets and clothing fabrics rely on ammonia as part of the finishing process but the most important use of ammonia is in in the manufacture of fertilisers.

(I can't think of the word ammonia without being instantly reminded of a Happy Harmonies cartoon from 1936 called 'Bottles' that has animated bottles singing a song that includes the lyrics 'Spirits of ammonia, things that creep up on ya.')

The Haber process was first demonstrated in the summer of 1909 by the German scientist Fritz Haber and his assistant Robert Le Rossignol. It was quickly purchased by the German chemical company BASF and they assigned the German chemist and engineer Carl Bosch the task of scaling up the machinery for industrial level production. Demand for nitrates and ammonia for use as fertilisers and feed stocks had been steadily increasing during the 19th century. The main source was from the mining of nitrate deposits, and the reserves were rapidly diminishing. The Haber process (sometimes also called the Haber-Bosch process) now produces in excess of 450 million tonnes of nitrogen fertiliser per year. In combination with pesticides, these fertilisers have quadrupled the productivity of agricultural land. Today nearly 80% of the nitrogen found in human tissue originated from the Haber process. Both Haber and Bosch were awarded Nobel prizes for their work in this field.

The Haber Process

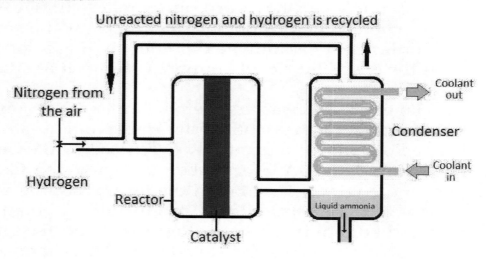

Hydrogenation and dehydrogenation

Hydrogenation is a chemical process based upon the chemical reaction that occurs when a compound or element has hydrogen added to it (by bonding pairs of hydrogen atoms to a molecule). The process requires a catalyst, most commonly nickel. Hydrocracking and the Haber process are examples of processes make use of this reaction, but it is more widely known as a way of converting unsaturated vegetable oils into saturated fats, similar to animal fats such as lard.

The resulting saturated oil fats are generally less expensive to produce than saturated animal fats and have a longer shelf life. This makes them ideal for use as shortening in most commercial baked goods. Solid or semi-solid fats are preferred for baking because the way they mix with flour produces a better texture in the end product.

The hydrogenation process can be accurately controlled to produce a wide range of consistencies. The major disadvantage of this is that by stopping the process before it is fully complete, some molecules are left in a transitionary condition. These are called trans-fats.

Trans-fats can occur naturally. They are irregularly shaped and the human body cannot process them in the way it can process fully saturated or unsaturated fats. This can cause health problems and, following legislation of varying degrees around the World, they are being phased out. Partially hydrogenated fats can be replaced by blending different oils, for example adding palm oil to unsaturated rich oils or even partially hydrogenated oils.

Fuel Cells

Although fuel cells have been in use for quite a while now, they are becoming more popular due to the ever improving technologies and processes being developed, and the fact that they produce no CO_2. Solar panels (discussed later on) are also in the same position and I believe that these two renewable technologies are the most likely to become mainstream.

Now, let's be clear about power generation. Combustion processes like gas turbines and internal combustion engines burn fuel and use the pressure generated by the subsequent expansion of gases to do mechanical work (pushing pistons up and down in car engines for example), which is used to produce either mechanical forces or generate electricity. The by-product, or waste gases, are pollutants such as carbon dioxide, and heat.

Batteries convert chemical energy into electrical energy. They have a fixed life span and then have to be discarded (which creates a problem because they contain toxic chemicals and acids). Re-chargeable batteries have become an everyday feature of modern life but even so, they need to be recharged using electricity generated by some other method. They also generate heat. Boeing's 787 Dreamliner was grounded for three months in 2013 due to problems including fires caused by the lithium-ion batteries originally used, and over- heating is not uncommon in mobile phones and other modern gadgets.

Fuel cells are devices that generate electricity through electrochemical processes instead of by combustion. They operate quietly and eficiently and produce virtually no pollutants. Fuel cells require a continuous source of fuel and oxygen or air to sustain the chemical reaction, and produce electricity for as long as fuel and air are fed into them. The by-products (emissions or waste gases) are water, heat and, in some cases, trace amounts of nitrous oxide (NO_2), also known as laughing gas.

There are various types of fuel cell, but they all work on the same basic principle. Each individual cell has two electrodes: one positive (cathode) and one negative (anode). The reactions that produce electricity occur at the electrodes. The cell also requires an electrolyte, which can be solid or liquid. The electrolyte is a substance that will only allow the desired type of ion to pass between the electrodes. It is vitally important because if other substances or free electrons reach the electrodes the reaction is disrupted and the eficiency of the cell decreases.

The anode and cathode contain catalysts that make the fuel oxidise. This creates positively charged protons (hydrogen ions) and negatively charged electrons. The protons are drawn through the electrolyte and the electrons move from the anode to the cathode through an external circuit, which produces Direct Current (DC) electricity. At the cathode the protons, electrons and oxygen react to form water.

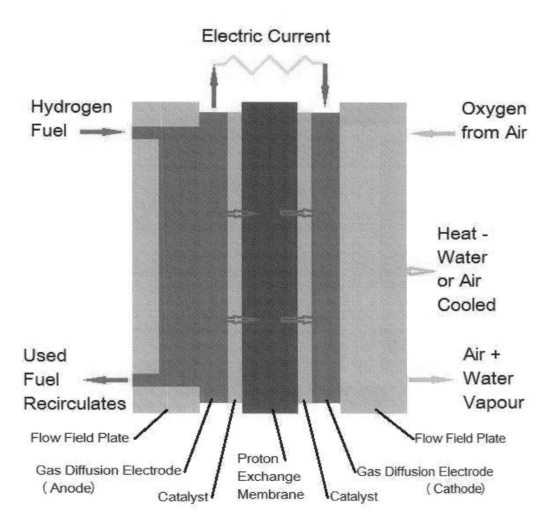

PEM Fuel Cell

The individual fuel cells are stacked together to form a fuel stack. There are seven distinct types of fuel cell that each have their own advantages and drawbacks. Here is a list followed by a more detailed look at how they work and what they are most suitable for.

Polymer Exchange Membrane Fuel Cell (PEMFC)
Solid Oxide Fuel Cell (SOFC)
Alkaline Fuel Cell (AFC)
Molten-Carbonate Fuel Cell (MCFC)
Phosphoric-Acid Fuel Cell (PAFC)
Direct-Methanol Fuel Cell (DMFC)
Microbial Fuel Cell (MFC)

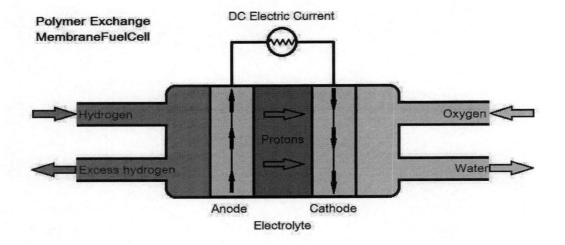

This uses a water based acidic polymer membrane as the electrolyte and platinum based electrodes. Because of the properties of the electrolyte and precious metals in the electrodes, this type of fuel cell needs pure hydrogen to operate. This means that there has to be less than 50 parts per million of contaminants such as carbon monoxide (CO). The oxygen can be either purified or extracted directly from the air at the electrode.

PEMFCs generate a relatively low level of heat (less than 100° C) and can be used as an 'on demand' system, which increases the overall eficiency of the system.

By changing the electrolyte from water based to a mineral acid based solution you can create a High Temperature PEMFC. These variants can operate at higher temperatures (up to 200° C), which overcomes some of the limitations of fuel purity – they can tolerate impurities of up 5% CO by volume – and are less complex. Drawbacks include lower power density and the fact that they need to be heated before use, whereas standard PEMFCs can be used from cold.

The average overall eficiency ratings are between 40% and 60% (The eficiency rating is the amount of fuel that is converted to useable power). PEMFCs are currently the leading technology for powering light duty vehicles (cars, motorbikes, vans, buses, etc.).

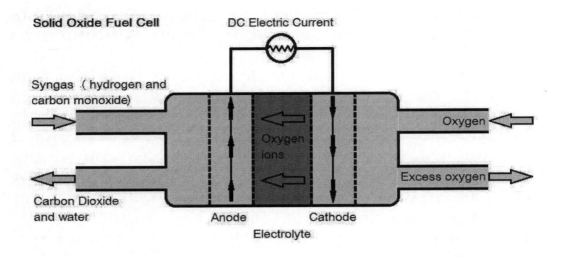

Solid Oxide Fuel Cell

DC Electric Current

Syngas (hydrogen and carbon monoxide)

Oxygen ions

Oxygen

Excess oxygen

Carbon Dioxide and water

Anode

Cathode

Electrolyte

Solid Oxide Fuel Cells use a solid ceramic based electrolyte instead of a liquid or membrane. They operate at very high temperatures, typically 800° C to 1,000° C. This high temperature means that fuels can be reformed within the fuel cell system, which enables them to use a wide variety of hydrocarbon fuels including coal gas. Another advantage is that the reaction rate increases to the point where metal catalysts are not needed for the electrodes.

Disadvantages are that they take longer to start up and reach operating temperature, must be made from robust heat-resistant materials and require shielding to prevent heat loss.

Although the overall eficiency of SOFCs is around 60%, this can be increased to 80% overall by harnessing the energy from the heat they produce.

SOFCs can be used for large and small stationary power generation, from 100kw off grid generators to Combined Heat and Power (CHP) systems for use in domestic situations.

They are also being developed for use as small portable chargers.

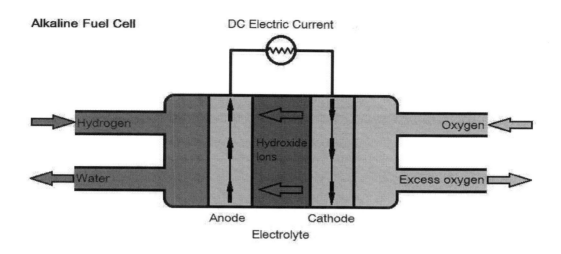

Alkaline Fuel Cell
DC Electric Current
Hydrogen
Hydroxide Ions
Oxygen
Water
Excess oxygen
Anode
Cathode
Electrolyte

AFCs were one of the first fuel cells to be developed and NASA used them to produce both electricity and water aboard spacecraft including the Space Shuttle.

As the name suggests, AFCs use an alkaline electrolyte and require pure hydrogen for fuel. Early cells had an operating temperature of over 100° C but the latest ones operate at around 70°C. This means that the traditional platinum (used because it outperforms other catalysts) can be replaced by a variety of non-precious (and therefore cheaper) catalysts, usually nickel. They have a high rate of chemical reaction and therefore the fuel to electricity conversion eficiency can be as high as 60%.

AFCs are currently the cheapest cells to manufacture but are prone to carbon dioxide poisoning (a build-up of CO2 around the anode and cathode) that reduces their eficiency.

The latest technical advances in fuel cell research have overcome this problem and AFCs are now being developed for commercial use. This should lead to wider use in the transport industry. Previously they have been used in space vehicles and underwater exploration vessels.

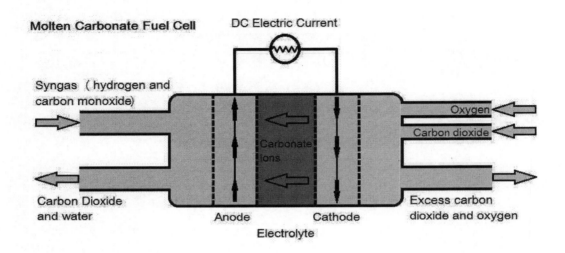

These use a molten carbonate salt solution in a porous ceramic matrix as the electrolyte. They operate at high temperatures, typically 650° C, which gives them the same advantages as SOFCs and enables them to achieve similar levels of eficiency.

Early MCFCs suffered from high temperature corrosion and the corrosive nature of the electrolyte but the latest versions have this under control and thus have a practical lifetime. MCFCs can be used in a stationary facility to generate large amounts of electricity in the order of megawatts. They are also practical for use in CHP systems.

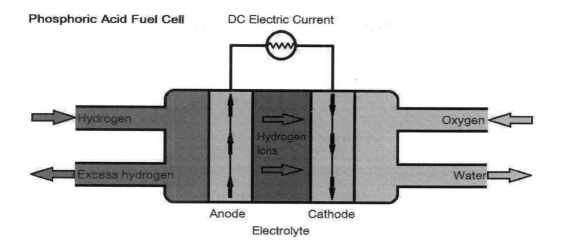

Phosphoric Acid Fuel Cell

The electrodes in this type of fuel cell are made of a carbon core with a light coating of platinum as the catalyst. The electrolyte is phosphoric acid that is contained in a silicon carbide structure. Most fuel cell units sold before 2001 used this technology. As standard they are the least energy eficient of all the fuel cell types but their operating temperature of about 180° C means that the heat can be harnessed for co-generation, which can raise their overall eficiency as high as 80%.

PAFCs are used for stationary power generation in the 100 to 400kw range (mostly for commercial purposes). They are also being developed for use in large vehicles such as trucks and buses.

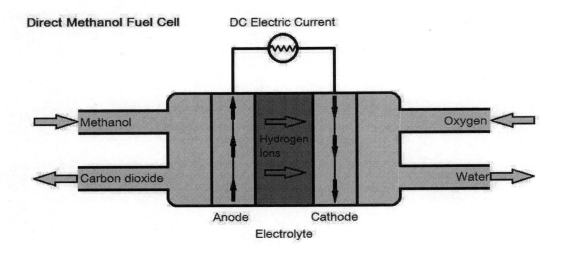

Direct Methanol Fuel Cell — DC Electric Current — Methanol — Oxygen — Hydrogen Ions — Carbon dioxide — Water — Anode — Cathode — Electrolyte

These were developed in the 1990's by researchers in several U.S. institutions including NASA and the Jet Propulsion Laboratory (JPL). They use a polymer membrane electrolyte and are similar to PEMFCs but use a platinum-ruthenium (a chemical element, symbol Ru, atomic number 44) catalyst on the anode. This enables it to draw hydrogen directly from liquid methanol.

Methanol is inexpensive and can be easily transported and stored. It has a relatively high energy density and is useable in a liquid reservoir (that can be topped up) or a cartridge (that is replaced when empty).

DMFCs operate in a temperature range from 60° C to 130° C and have an overall eficiency of about 30%. They are currently used in applications that have modest power requirements such as chargers or portable power packs. They are also used to power materials handling vehicles such as fork lift trucks. Conventionally, fork lift trucks run on rechargeable batteries. Switching to fuel cells saves time in refuelling (minutes instead of hours for recharging) and frees up the space required for the battery storage and infrastructure.

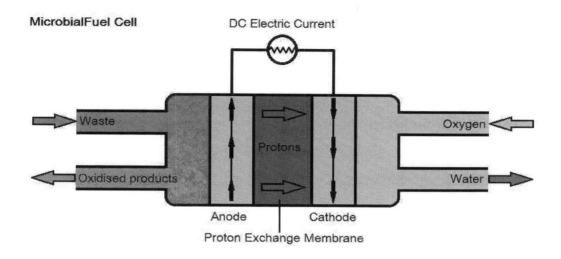

MicrobialFuel Cell

DC Electric Current

Waste

Oxygen

Protons

Oxidised products

Water

Anode

Cathode

Proton Exchange Membrane

Microbial fuel cells are different from all the others in that they use living bio-catalysts instead of chemical catalysts. Although the idea has been around for about 100 years, it was not until 1999 that a scientific breakthrough enabled practical microbial fuel cells to be made.

MFCs use the process of cellular respiration. This is what cells use to convert nutrients into a substance called Adenosine Triphosphate (ATP), which is the fuel used for cellular activity. Bacterial respiration is the oxidisation and reduction of organic molecules and this process naturally moves lots of electrons around.

The big breakthrough in 1999 involved the use of a recently discovered type of micro-organism called exoelectrogens. These are a special class of bacteria that will stick to the surface of an anode coated with a specialised protein and then transfer electrons to it.

Organic fuel enters the anode chamber and the bacteria get to work converting it to ATP. The by-products of this process are protons, electrons and CO2. The electrons are accepted into the anode while the protons pass through a proton exchange membrane into the cathode chamber. An oxidising agent recombines the electrons from the cathode with hydrogen and produces water.

The eficiency of MFCs can be up to 50% and this is expected to improve as further research is completed. They typically operate at between 20° C and 40° C. The conditions of a waste water treatment plant are ideal for the bacteria that can be used. The energy produced offsets the cost of running the plant and the bacteria eat up around 80% of the sludge present in waste water. The latest developments produce clean water, electricity and methane, which can be used as a clean fuel.

Five general advantages of fuel cells over conventional power sources

1) Eficiency

Energy eficiency is basically the amount of useable energy produced using a specific unit of fuel. Below is a list of the major methods of energy production currently in use, with their eficiency levels.

Fuel Cells: Between 40% and 80% depending on type

Diesel ICE: Up to 20% for modern engines (typically 15% to 18%)

Petrol ICE: Up to 20% for modern engines (typically 12% to 16%)

Wind Power: 40% to 45% in optimal conditions. Usually a lot less

Nuclear Conversion: Around 38% for the thermal cycle but only 0.7% for overall energy conversion.

Coal Fired: Typically 35% to 40%

Natural Gas: Typically 35% to 40% but the latest technology can achieve up to 60%.

Hydro-electric: 85% to 90%.

Geo-thermal: Around 35%

2) Fuel cells, hydro-electric, geothermal, solar, wind, wave and tidal power are the only methods of generating power that don't produce pollutants and dangerous by-products.

3) Fuel cells require just a little bit of simple maintenance due to the fact that they have very few moving parts.

4) There is little or no noise pollution when using fuel cells. In fact most of them produce no audible noise.

5) Using stationary fuel cells to generate power at the point of use would enable a decentralised power grid that is more stable and allow power on demand for everyone.

5 Where are we now?

The world is taking the first proper steps towards a sustainable hydrogen economy that will bring huge benefits to mankind. As we progress further along this path and combine it with other forms of green and renewable energy the amount of pollution will drop dramatically and the quality of the air, particularly in large cities, will improve, bringing with it a decrease in respiratory and other health problems.

The main emphasis at the moment is on introducing hydrogen powered vehicles but it is also being used to generate electricity as an alternative to diesel generators. First of all though, the hydrogen has to be produced.

Generating or manufacturing hydrogen fuel

As the concept and reality of using hydrogen as a fuel are gaining momentum, there are many projects taking place in universities and research centres looking into ways of producing hydrogen cleanly and cheaply. Here are some of the most promising ones.

USC – University of Southern California

I have singled out this university because of its extremely illustrious history and importance in developing technologies.

USC is a private, non-profit and non-sectarian research university founded in 1880. The main campus is in Los Angeles and it is California's oldest private research university. It quickly became an engine for economic activity and contributes billions of dollars into the economy of Los Angeles County every year. It also has links with many top research facilities worldwide.

Chemists at the USC Loker Hydrocarbon Research Institute have found a way of producing hydrogen by recycling carbon dioxide through a process of dehydrogenation of formic acid. The breakthrough over other similar research is that the catalyst they have developed releases hydrogen without producing any polluting by-products.

Formic acid occurs naturally in the venom of bee and ant stings, and through the decay of vegetation. The fact that is can also be made by reacting carbon dioxide with hydrogen makes it an appealing option for scientists as a carrier and storage reservoir for hydrogen.

The breakthrough made at USC Loker is the development of a new iridium based catalyst to release the hydrogen. This catalyst has some major advantages: it doesn't degenerate when exposed to air and is almost inexhaustibly re-usable.

Professor Travis J. Williams, lead author of the study, is on record as stating, 'We think it may never die. We've demonstrated it through 2.2 million turnovers over several months. At that point, the catalyst was still alive but we were bored with the experiment. This would be a big money save for anyone who wants to generate and store hydrogen as a fuel.'

They used 'neat' formic acid (with no added water or solvent) because when you release energy from a liquid fuel you want to have as little unnecessary mass as possible.

Think of it this way: If there is twice as much fuel in a gallon of liquid then your vehicle will go twice as far on each tank of fuel.

The concept is basically the reverse of combustion. It takes the CO2 released as a result of burning carbon based fuels and turns it into a useable non-polluting fuel.

This development will essentially lead to a 'hydrogen on demand' system that produces hydrogen directly for a linked fuel cell to generate electricity or straight into an internal combustion engine designed to run on hydrogen. So far all the indications are that this process is inherently both safe and sustainable.

Large Scale Manufacturing

There are many companies around the world that manufacture hydrogen already. More research and resources are being put into supplying hydrogen (and other fuels for use in fuel cells) all the time. The major downside to this approach is that the fuel has to be transported to the point of use, usually by pipeline or in cylinders.

On Site Generation

There is a lot of interest in producing hydrogen on site for re-fuelling fuel cell vehicles (FCEVs) and the number of companies able to provide this equipment is increasing rapidly.

One important pan-European project called Hydrogen for Innovative Vehicles (HyFive) is rolling out FCEVs and the required re-fuelling infrastructure. In May 2016 the first London HyFive hydrogen re-fuelling station opened in Teddington. It uses ITM Power H Fuel hydrogen generating stations that run on electricity to generate hydrogen by electrolysis, which is then compressed and stored to be dispensed on demand. It needs a water supply as well as the electricity and if the electricity comes from a renewable or green energy source then the entire process, including running the FCEVs, is carbon free. Currently, their highest capacity unit produces enough hydrogen fuel for 94 vehicle refills every 24 hours.

An interesting article caught my eye – there might be oceans of hydrogen gas trapped under the World's oceans. If this is correct it would be a major game changer.

Hydrogen fuel vehicles

There are currently three FCEV models available to own or lease in the U.K., the Hyundai ix35 Fuel Cell and the Toyota Mirai. Honda launched their latest Clarity Fuel Cell in late 2016 and most of the major car manufacturers will be introducing FCEVs in the next few years including BMW, the Audi group (including Volkswagen) and Mercedes Benz. There are also some start-up companies preparing to join in, such as Riversimple. At the same time, they are starting to scale back on the production of diesel powered vehicles.

How do fuel cell cars work?

So, we know what fuel cells are, the different types and how they work. Hydrogen fuel cell technology is an area of the automotive industry that is becoming increasingly important, with manufacturers committing to developing FCEVs.

The most common fuel cell for powering vehicles at the moment is PEM. Many individual cells are combined into a fuel cell stack to generate the required voltage. As we have already discussed, the by product is water.

At this point, rather than try to explain how a fuel cell vehicle works in detail, I suggest that you follow these three links. I thoroughly recommend the video located near the bottom of the Toyota page.

Toyota
Honda

<u>Hyundai</u>

Here is a summary of the process, mostly written to give me something to do while you visited the websites and watched the videos.

Basically, there is a hydrogen fuel tank, a fuel cell stack, oxygen intake, electric motors and possibly a storage battery. Hydrogen from the tank and oxygen from the air flow into the fuel stack, which produces electricity to drive the motors. Usually there is a motor for each wheel, so the car is four wheel drive. Most will also use regenerative braking to put electricity back into the system as well. The by-product of the fuel cells is water, which is released into the environment. Currently FCEVs have a range of 300 to 350 miles per tank of hydrogen and the re-fuelling time is three to five minutes, comparable to current petrol and diesel vehicles. Because it is also a mobile electricity generator, the vehicle can be fitted with a power output socket and could be used to run electrical appliances of all descriptions. So, you could go camping and have a TV, cooker, lights, etc. powered by your car.

Other vehicles

<u>Buses</u>

There are many start-up programs around the World using fuel cells to power buses (FCEB). The first FCEB was demonstrated in 1993. FCEB technology reduces emissions and will achieve better fuel economy than conventional diesel powered buses.

According to the U.S.A.'s Federal Transit Administration (FTA) who have been running assessments and development programs on FCEB for a number of years under their <u>American Fuel Cell Bus Project</u>, every single FCEB has the potential to reduce the amount of carbon dioxide released into the atmosphere by 100 tons per year and eliminate the need for 9,000 gallons of fuel every year over the life cycle of the vehicle. This translates into savings of $37,000 per vehicle annually over conventional diesel fuel buses. They are also quieter and smoother, especially when idling or stationary. As my daughter said when I told her about them, you would be able to rest your head against the window without having your teeth rattled loose when the vehicle is stationary.

In Europe we had the CHIC project (Clean Hydrogen in European Cities). This was a major project deploying fleets of FCEBs and associated hydrogen fuelling stations. Its main aims are to enhance and develop FCEB technology and provide a way for European cities to run pollution free public transport.

CHIC had many partners, including Transport for London, Daimler, Total, Shell and The University of Stuttgart. There were eight demonstration sites in use, including Berlin, Cologne, Hamburg, Milan and London, with related projects in Rotterdam, London, Antwerp, Cherbourg, Rome, Aberdeen, San Remo and Stuttgart.

There are other projects around the World as well, including Australia, Japan and China.

In late 2016 London Mayor Sadiq Khan is quoted as saying, "I want London to become a world leader in hydrogen and electric bus technology. I'm implementing hard-hitting measures to clean up London's toxic air and it's great that more cities are getting on board to phase out the procurement of pure diesel buses, which sends a clear signal that only the cleanest technologies are wanted in our cities." The mayor of Copenhagen, Frank Jensen, added: "In Copenhagen, all new buses will be based on zero-emission and low-noise technologies from 2019."

The governments of eleven big cities (Amsterdam, Cape Town, Copenhagen, Los Angeles, New York, San Francisco and others) responded to Khan's call and have decided to stop purchasing diesel-only buses by the end of 2020. Madrid, Mexico-City and Paris assured that they will remove any diesel version from their cities by 2025. All in all, the number of fuel cell buses in use Europe-wide is set to increase to around 300 to 400 in the next few years. South Tyrol alone intends to buy ten to fifteen new hydrogen buses after CHIC has run out. The state government has already approved the EUR 8.5 million needed for the project.

Meanwhile, Japan is sparing no effort to prepare thoroughly for the 2020 Olympics. They are aiming to have one hundred hydrogen-driven buses running in Tokyo by then.

Hydrail

Short for Hydrogen Rail, this is a generic term referring to rail based transportation that uses hydrogen as fuel, including vehicles such as trams as well as railway locomotives. China has two Hydrail trains in operation right now and there are many projects underway to replace diesel locomotives. Japan, China and Europe appear to be the most committed to this technology.

Internal Combustion

Apparently, most modern internal combustion engines (ICEs) can be converted to run on hydrogen, and even be switchable from hydrogen back to petrol if there is no hydrogen refuelling available. It is mostly about getting the engine management correct and installing the hydrogen fuel tank.

An ICE designed specifically for hydrogen is much more eficient though, and there is less chance of it going wrong. Research shows that the power output of a direct injected hydrogen engine is about 20% higher than an equivalent petrol engine. Direct injection engines put out about 40% more power than those using a carburettor.

Hydrogen hybrid ICEs, either using hydrogen from a refillable tank or an on demand system using electrolysis, combine the hydrogen with the petrol or diesel fuel/air mixture before it enters the engine.

As much as 60% of the fuel in a standard ICE is lost as heat. Introducing hydrogen makes a cleaner fuel burn that reduces engine and exhaust gas temperatures and improves power and eficiency.

Aston Martin entered an HH powered Rapide S in the 2010 Nurburgring 24 hours race and finished second in the SP8 class. It was the first car to compete in the race using hydrogen fuel. Alset Global, the company that developed the HH technology engine, won the Powertrain of The Year award at the Professional Motorsport World Expo held in Cologne in 2013.

What I would really like to see is motorsport switching to hydrogen ICEs. The potential is enormous and would drive the development for consumer use. There would still be the noise associated with motorsport, which is a drawback with the electric racing formulas such as Formula E, and I'm convinced that most petrol-heads would become hydrogen-heads very easily. Imagine Formula 1 using loud powerful V8, 10 or 12 cylinder hydrogen ICE powertrains. I'm sure that would generate much more interest than the current hybrid technology.

Aeroplanes

According to the Guinness Book of Records website, the first manned hydrogen powered aircraft was a two seat Dimona motor glider using fuel cells to power an electric motor which drove the propeller. The flights took place at an airfield in Ocana, southern Spain between February and March 2008.

On September 29th 2016, a twin cabin plane called HY4 was successfully tested by German engineers at Stuttgart airport. The flight test of the World's first four seater hydrogen powered aircraft lasted ten minutes. Developed by aircraft maker Pipistrel, fuel cell specialist Hydrogenics, the University of Ulm and the German Aerospace Centre DLR, the HY4 uses emission-free hybrid fuel cells to generate electricity from hydrogen, which powers the aircraft during flight. Batteries are used for take-off and landing. It has a range of up to 1,500km (930 miles) at a cruising speed of 165 kph (102 mph).

The aircraft industry is searching for ways to reduce emissions and both Boeing and Airbus have tested smaller fuel cell planes in recent years.

There are still issues with running jet engines using hydrogen as a fuel, but a company called Reaction Engines has been working on a new type of engine. Called SABRE, it works in two different configurations.

In Air Breathing Mode, the rocket engine sucks in atmospheric air as a source of oxygen (the same as a jet engine) and uses it to burn with the on-board liquid hydrogen fuel in the rocket combustion chamber. Above the atmosphere it switches to Conventional Rocket mode and uses oxygen from an on-board storage tank.

The SABRE engine in Air Breathing Mode gives an eight-fold improvement in propellant consumption over conventional rockets. In this mode it can operate at over five times the speed of sound and up to an altitude of twenty-five km.

Above this height it switches to Conventional Rocket Mode which enables it to power the vehicle into Earth orbit. This does away with the need for multi-stage launch vehicles.

There are currently two aircraft projects being developed for the SABRE engine.

LAPCAT 2 is a concept for a hypersonic airliner capable of taking up to 300 passengers that would be able to fly from

London to Sydney in less than six hours. It will use a development of the SABRE engine called SCIMITAR that runs in air breathing mode only.

SKYLON is a concept for a re-usable spaceplane using SABRE engines. It will take off and land as a conventional aircraft and be able to deliver up to fifteen tonnes of payload into low Earth orbit. (Basically a real version of the Pan Am shuttle from the film 2001).

Here is a link to the Reaction Engine website for the latest developments.

Hydrogen Powered Ships

The world's first hydrogen-powered ship was launched on 29th August 2008. The FCS Alsterwasser, developed by the German company Alster-Touristik GmbH, uses fuel cells and a lead gel battery designed by **Proton Motor**

The general term for ships powered by green or renewable technology is Zem (Zero emission) Ships. The general consensus in the maritime industry is that switching to hydrogen power is viable, and there are various projects underway. The major stumbling block at the moment is the same as the other transport systems – cost and availability of fuel, but this is gradually being resolved.

Bristol Hydrogen Boats and Auriga Energy teamed up to produce the U.K.'s first fuel cell ferry. Called Hydrogenesis, it carries twelve passengers and operates in Bristol between Temple Quay and the SS Great Britain. £225,000 was funded by Bristol City council and the vessel won the Environmental Innovation of The Year award in 2011.

Bristol, by the way, has been steadily investing in energy eficiency and renewable energy and won the European Green Capital award in 2015. More details of the winners since its launch in 2010 can be found on the **European Commission site.**

Liquid Hydrogen – The Fuel of Choice for Space Exploration

All current space launch vehicles use rocket technology. In combination with an oxidiser (normally liquid oxygen), liquid hydrogen gives the highest eficiency in relation to the amount of propellant used (specific impulse) of any known propellant.

Fuel cells are used to provide electricity for human spaceflight. Originally alkaline cells were used, from the Gemini missions through to the Space Shuttle and International Space Station (ISS). Now they are switching to PEMFCs which are becoming more powerful, lighter, safer, simpler to operate and increasingly reliable.

Static Generation

Uninterruptible Power Supply (UPS)

This is an apparatus that provides emergency power when the mains power fails. They are typically used to protect hardware such as computers, data centres, telecommunications equipment, medical equipment and any other electrical equipment where an unexpected power disruption could cause injuries, fatalities, serious business disruption or data loss.

They work by supplying energy stored in batteries, superconductors or flywheels nearly instantaneously in the event of a power failure. They need to be able to supply power for long enough to enable an emergency power system or standby generator to start up or for the protected equipment to be safely shut down.

A Line-interactive UPS adds a special type of transformer that enables it to automatically filter any power supply fluctuations to provide stable power to the user.

Hydrogen UPS systems are now available that use PEM fuel cells. Upon grid power interruption the fuel cell takes up the load with the help of a storage battery during the first few minutes of operation.

Emergency power system/Backup generator

These are the next stage of a UPS. Most backup generators run using a petrol or diesel generator but these are gradually being replaced by fuel cell generators. Compared to diesel generators, fuel cells can provide savings of up to seventy-five percent, are almost silent when in operation and the only exhaust is water vapour.

Independent Power Supply

Hydrogen fuel cell generators can be used to power homes and buildings completely independently from a national power grid. When combined with other technologies such as solar panels, you can have a system that generates hydrogen which is then used to refuel both your car and your home power system. There are many projects around the world developing this technology.

The best way to store energy is to generate hydrogen gas via electrolyzers with solar energy and pure water during the day. Electrolyzers produce hydrogen gas by using an electric current to separate water into its composite gases: hydrogen and oxygen.

During night or when additional energy is required, the hydrogen is used to produce power with a fuel cell. Storage batteries take the very fast and short loads, while the massive permanent energy load is supplied by the hydrogen fuel cell.

Combining different power sources and storage techniques into a cohesive process will revolutionize the power industry, as most domestic applications will be self-sustaining and do away with the need for a centralized power grid. The benefits will be felt the most in poorer countries and remote locations.

II Other clean energy production methods

6 Solar Energy

There are two ways of converting sunlight into electricity: Concentrated Solar Power (CSP) and Photovoltaic (PV).

Concentrated Solar Power

This uses lenses or mirrors and tracking systems to focus a large area of sunlight into a small beam. It collects heat and uses that to create steam to generate electricity. There are four main types;

Solar Tower

Also known as central receivers, these use flat mirrors to focus sunlight onto a central tower. This heats up a liquid (usually molten salt) which creates steam for use in electricity generation. Solar Towers are more efficient and cost effective than other CSPs and also provide better energy storage capability.

There are currently around ten of this type of CSP in use around the world, mostly in hot and dry locations such as California, Spain, Africa, China, Australia and India.

In Israel, the Ashalim Solar Thermal Power Station is being built in the Negev desert. Due to be completed in late 2017, this will be the world's largest CSP. Covering a staggering one million square metres covered with fifty-five thousand mirrors concentrated onto a 240 m high tower (the World's tallest), it is expected to generate 320 GW of electricity, which is enough to power 120,000 homes.

Once completed, the Ashalim Solar Thermal Power Station will save 110,000 tons of CO_2 emissions per year. It is part of a project that aims to have 10% of Israel's electricity generated by renewables by 2020. Here is an interesting article about Israel's energy generation history and policy.

Parabolic Trough

As you have probably surmised from the title, this design of CSP uses curved mirrors that concentrate the sun's energy at a central focal point. It works at all levels from very small scale, where it can be used to heat food and liquids, to large scale.

There are around fifty large scale Parabolic Troughs in use around the world with more under construction. Large scale Parabolic Troughs use a tube (usually a Dewar Tube, which is insulated in a similar fashion to a vacuum flask) that runs along the focal point. The liquid inside it is heated by the reflected sunlight and can be used in a heat engine to generate power or to directly drive machinery. Efficiency ratings for this method are currently comparable to Photo Voltaic methods.

Fresnel Reflectors

These are made of thin, flat mirror strips that concentrate sunlight onto tubes to heat a liquid which is then used to generate power. Flat mirrors allow for more reflective surface than parabolic reflectors, capture more of the available sunlight and are cheaper to manufacture. Operating and maintaining them is relatively easy and this is an emerging technology that could potentially replace Solar Towers and Parabolic Troughs as it also has the best land to electricity ratio of any CSP. This is mostly due to the fact that the land beneath it can still be used for agriculture.

Overall, CSP is a promising technology but is limited due to the need for large areas of land and high concentrations of sunlight. Having said that, however, large facilities situated in and around desert areas could be used to add a lot of electricity to national and international power grids.

Photovoltaic (PV)

PV applies to systems that work by converting light into electricity using semiconducting materials.

The photovoltaic effect is a phenomenon that is being continuously studied around the world, especially in the fields of physics, photochemistry and electrochemistry. A typical PV system uses solar panels (made up of small solar cells) that generate electrical power. This method does not generate any pollutants. PV systems have been in use for over fifty years, mostly in specialised applications such as power systems for satellites and spacecraft. In the last twenty years they have been introduced more generally in standalone and grid connected systems. The technology and manufacturing of PV systems is advancing rapidly and over 100 countries now use it in some capacity. It is currently the third largest renewable energy source worldwide, after Hydro Electric and Wind Power.

Okay, I hear you ask, how does PV work? Well, to start with let's find out what the photovoltaic effect is.

It was discovered by a French physicist called Edmund Becquerel in 1839. What he found is that some materials produce a small electric current when exposed to sunlight.

Solar cells are small devices that convert sunlight into electricity. They consist of two wafer thin layers of silicon crystal, called P-type and N-Type. The P-type have been heated to make them attract electrons. The N-type is placed on top and has been treated to make it release electrons. When sunlight hits the N-type layer, it excites the electrons and this gives them enough energy to move. The electrons then flow into the P-type layer and generate an electrical current.

Electrical contacts are added to both the top and bottom layers and a protective layer and anti-reflective coating are added to the top. Solar panels produce DC current, so for domestic use they are connected to an inverter that changes the current to AC.

Solar Cell Structure

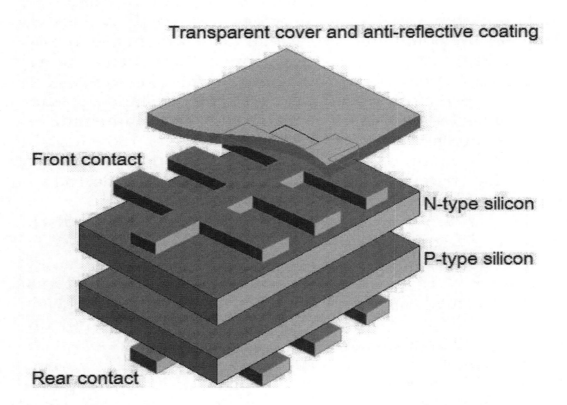

Transparent cover and anti-reflective coating

Front contact

N-type silicon

P-type silicon

Rear contact

Solar cell process

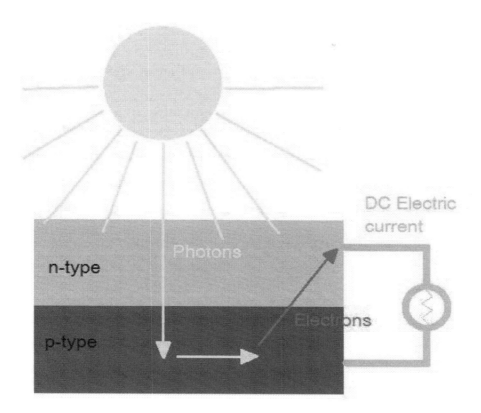

A solar panel (or module) is made up of several solar cells connected together and fitted into a frame, which produces a larger amount of power.

A solar array is several solar panels connected together, which increases the power output further.

A lot of research is being channelled into the development of new materials and methods to increase the e🔧ciency of PV units. The most promising area of research is Organic Solar Cells (also referred to as plastic solar cells). These offer easier and cheaper manufacturing and more flexibility in the construction of solar panels.

The most exciting recent advances are the ability to print solar cells and panels and the use of Perovskite. These will make PV cells increasingly cheaper and more efficient. As far as PV is concerned, the future looks very bright indeed (sorry, but I just had to put that in!).

7 Hydro power

This term applies to power derived from the energy of fast flowing or falling water.

Throughout history, the power of flowing water has been used to provide energy for mechanical devices that were used for a variety of tasks including flour and other mills, early manufacturing, and pumps for irrigation purposes. Although most of these methods were later powered by steam and then electricity or internal combustion engines, the development of turbines led to the introduction of water powered electricity generation, or hydroelectric power.

A conventional dammed hydroelectric generator is the most common source, but 'run of the river' installations are in use that use a smaller dam, or do away with it completely. There are also pumped storage facilities where, at low demand periods, water is pumped from a low level reservoir to a higher one, where it is stored until needed to produce more electricity at peak times.

In an order that depends on where you live, the most famous hydroelectric dams in the world are: the Three Gorges Dam on the Yangtze River in China, the Aswan Dam on the Nile River in Egypt and the Hoover Dam on the

Colorado River on the borders of the U.S.A. states of Nevada and Arizona. There are many other hydroelectric dams around the world.

China is by far the biggest generator of hydroelectricity. Brazil, Canada and the U.S.A. are a close match for second place, with Russia, Norway, India and South America a bit further down the list.

Things change a bit when you look at how much of the total electricity used in a country comes from hydroelectric sources. Norway generates 99% of the country's electricity this way and there is room for further development. There are plans in place for Norway to export electricity to neighbouring countries. (So if you live in Norway, give yourself a pat on the back for being so green and go and celebrate by riding a bike or buying an electric or FCEV car).

Other countries that generate more than 95% of their electricity using hydro power are (in no particular order) Zambia, Albania, Belize, Paraguay, Bhutan, Burma, Mozambique, Ethiopia, Lesotho and Iceland.

8 Energy from our seas and oceans

Wave Power

This is a method of harvesting the energy of waves in water (usually a sea or ocean) and putting that energy to useful work. This can be water desalination, powering pumps (to pump water into reservoirs for example), a few other applications and, most importantly, electricity generation. A machine that can make use of wave power is generally known as a Wave Energy Converter (WEC). Let's take a look at the four most common methods of extracting energy from waves currently being used.

Point Absorber Buoy

These devices are the most common form of what are termed Oscillating Wave Surge Converters. These devices float on the surface of the water, held in place by cables attached to the sea floor. The buoys use the rise and fall of the surface swells to drive hydraulic pumps that generate electricity.

Surface Attenuator

Similar to Point Absorber Buoys but with multiple floating segments connected to each other. The swells create a flexing motion that drives hydraulic pumps to generate electricity.

Oscillating Water Column

The swells compress air in an integrated chamber that forces air through a turbine to create electricity. The process of the air being forced through the turbines creates quite a lot of noise, making these the noisiest method of converting wave power.

Overtopping Device

These are long structures that use wave velocity to fill a reservoir to a higher level than the surrounding ocean. The greater height of the reservoir is used to run water through low-head turbines that generate electricity.

The European Marine Energy Centre (EMEC), based in Orkney in the U.K. is the first (and so far only) centre of its kind in the world to provide test sites and facilities for developers of both wave and tidal energy. A visit to their website is well worthwhile and I recommend the short video on their Marine Energy page.

Tidal Energy

This exploits the energy produced by the tidal waters. The power of these fast-flowing sea currents is often magnified by narrow channels in the sea bed, headlands, inlets and straits. There are many projects around the world and a variety of tidal energy converters.

9 Geothermal

Thermal energy is a natural process that generates heat and stores it near or on the surface of the Earth. The differences in temperature throughout the molten core of the planet carries heat towards the surface, where it heats the mantle (the covering of rock that forms the surface of the Earth). Geothermal energy production uses the energy stored by this process.

At a basic level, geothermal energy has been used by mankind since Palaeolithic times, through hot springs. The Romans also used it for heating buildings. Recently it has been harnessed to create geothermal electricity, in which the heat is used to create steam that drives a turbine to generate electricity in the same way that steam is used in nuclear power and fossil fuel generators.

Countries that have natural hot springs and geysers or are volcanically active can make use of this resource relatively easily. This includes parts of the U.S.A., Iceland, China and Japan. More recently, other areas have been opened up by new technologies. Geothermal energy is considered to be cost effective, reliable, sustainable and environmentally friendly.

For more details and the latest news, <u>this is a good site to visit</u>.

10 Biomass

Biomass is material from living or recently living organisms. In energy terms it often refers to plant based material but it can also mean animal or vegetable derived materials. Energy generated using biomass techniques is called 'Bioenergy'.

The material that is captured in fossil fuels is fossilised biomass, but using it returns CO_2 into the atmosphere that was captured millions of years ago. Using biomass returns CO_2 that has been absorbed very recently and is part of what is called 'The Carbon Cycle'.

'What's that? Some kind of expensive bicycle?' I hear you ask. No, of course not. It is basically the cycle of life on Earth. A series of processes combine to make carbon compounds that are released into the environment. Carbon Dioxide in the atmosphere is converted into living tissue by the process of photosynthesis. The CO_2 is returned to the atmosphere by respiration (breathing), the decay of dead organisms, and burning biomass.

There are five basic categories of material that can be used to generate energy. These are:

Virgin Wood from forestry, wood processing and arboreal activities.

Energy Crops – high yield crops grown specifically for energy applications.

Agricultural Residue which is the organic residue left after harvesting and processing.

Food Waste – food and drink manufacturing and consumer waste.

Industrial Waste– from manufacturing and industrial processes.

Biomass can be used to generate heat and electricity, liquid biofuel or combustible biogas. This is achieved by means of two methods; Thermal Conversion and Chemical Conversion.

Thermal Conversion

As the name suggests, this involves using heat to convert biomass into a different chemical form. The main processes are:

Combustion

Yes, setting fire to it is the simplest method of converting biomass to energy for use in space heating, heating a liquid (normally water) for central heating and other similar uses. It can also be used to generate steam for electricity generation.

Gasification

The same process described in the section about producing, processing and storing hydrogen.

Pyrolysis

This is the thermochemical decomposition of organic material in the absence of oxygen. It produces gases and liquids, leaving behind a carbon rich solid residue. Pyrolysis is the precursor to gasification and is used to produce charcoal, methanol, PVC, syngas and loads more. It also plays an important role in cooking – specifically baking, frying, grilling and caramelizing.

Chemical Conversion

This uses chemical reactions instead of heat. The main process is Biochemical Conversion, which uses bacteria or other micro-organisms that produce enzymes to break down the biomass. The main processes are:

Anaerobic Digestion (AD)

Bacteria break down organic material in the absence of air. This produces three things – biogas that contains methane, a solid residue similar to compost, and a liquor that can be used as a fertiliser. It has been used to process sewage since the 19th century.

Fermentation

This is the same process used in brewing and wine making. It converts sugars into alcohol and can be further distilled to obtain bio-methanol, which can be used as a fuel or added to petrol.

Composting

Similar to AD, this process used different bacteria. As any keen gardener will know, it also generates a lot of heat, which can be used to generate power through a heat pump.

Bioenergy currently generates around 100 gigawatts of power globally and provides around five percent of world transport fuel. You will use one of the by-products the next time you have a charcoal barbecue.

11 Nuclear power

This process uses nuclear reactions that release nuclear energy. The result of this is large amounts of heat that is most commonly used to drive steam turbines and produce electricity. It is a low carbon power generation method and produces very little CO_2. Since the process was first commercialised in the 1970's, about 65 billion tonnes of carbon dioxide that would have been produced using fossil fuels to generate the heat has been saved. It is also used to power large submarines.

Unfortunately, due to concerns about radioactive waste disposal, its possible use to make atomic weapons, and nuclear accidents such as Three Mile Island, Chernobyl and more recently Fukushima, there has been a lot of opposition to Nuclear Power. Modern reactors are much safer and more eficient than their predecessors and produce less waste. In 2012 the World Nuclear Association reported that nuclear electricity generation was at its lowest level since 1999. Things have improved since then, with over sixty-five new nuclear power plants currently under construction and one hundred and fifty or so more in the planning stages.

Of course, we are talking about the process of nuclear fission. There is much research being done into nuclear fusion, which is the process that takes place inside the sun. If this can be controlled and harnessed it will be one of the biggest breakthroughs in history.

12 Wind power

Harnessing the power of the wind has played a pivotal role in human history. Sailing, using wind propulsion to move craft over water, ice or land has been in use since at least 5,000 BC, when the first records of its use show sailing boats on the Nile River. The earliest representation of a sail ship is on a painted disc found in Kuwait, estimated to date from between 5,500 and 5,000 BC. All major civilisations since then have used it to explore, trade and supply their empires.

From the middle ages there was a steady progress in sailing technology, ship building and navigation, resulting in ever increasing exploration, the development of military and merchant navies, advances in naval warfare and vast amounts of trade. It is still very much in use today and has a large range of participants. Probably the best known sailing race is the Americas Cup.

Windmills are another early adoption of wind power. According to historical data, windmills were first used in China to pump water from around 2,000 BC. The Persians used them to pump water and mill grains from around 500 AD.

In Europe windmills used to crush grain began appearing from around 1100 AD. In the 1300's the Dutch used windmills to drain water from low-lying regions. With the invention of steel blades, windmill use exploded in the late 1890's for pumping water and generating electricity and they were used extensively in the settling of the U.S.A. and Australia.

A lot of the electricity generation and pumping was taken over by steam engines and internal combustion but the use of wind power has remained quite strong. Interest peaked during the oil crisis in the early 1970's, along with a more general interest in renewable and alternative energy sources. Wind turbines have been continuously developed and improved since then, assisted by various government incentives (including tax credits) in different countries around the world for renewable energy production.

Modern wind turbines are complicated pieces of machinery. There are currently two basic types of wind turbine – vertical-axis, most often associated with the Darrieus model, which resembles a whisk or eggbeater, and the more commonly used horizontal-axis, which include the traditional windmills and modern three blade wind turbines. Groups (or arrays) of wind turbines are called wind farms and this is the most widespread usage of them. Wind farms can be on or off shore and generate electricity that is put into energy grids for large scale consumer purposes.

The main components of a wind turbine are;

A tower that supports the rest of the structure;

A drive train that includes a gearbox and generator;

The blades (or rotors) that convert the wind energy into rotational energy that drives the generator.

Other equipment including controllers for adjusting the blade pitch and direction, pumps and lubrication, electrical cables, ground support and interconnection facilities.

Wind turbines come in a variety of sizes and power ratings. A small individual use turbine stands around 30 feet high with rotors between 8 and 25 feet in diameter while the largest ones (used in offshore facilities) are 20 storeys high with rotors up to around 380 feet in diameter (slightly longer than a football pitch).

The total wind powered generating capacity globally is now over 435 GW, which is enough to supply in the region of 350 million households. The global growth rate is currently around 17%.

For more information, here are two useful links.

The U.S.A. Government site

Wind Europe

III Advantages and disadvantages

13 Large scale energy production (for power grids)

Solar Towers

These require desert or semi desert conditions and will, therefore, require the electricity generated to be transmitted over quite large distances. This means that some of the power is lost before it gets into the grid. A major advantage in their location is that it is land that is very difficult to use for any other purpose and there are no large local populations that will be adversely affected by their construction and use.

Because this is a relatively new technology that is still being developed, requires large amounts of land and large structures, it is expensive to set up.

Although it requires strong sunlight, this method continues to generate power for a while after the sun has set due to the inbuilt heat energy storage capacity. Once it has been running for a short period of time the electricity production costs are quite low, especially when combined with the latest storage batteries.

So, for the regions of the world where the conditions are right, this is a practical long term technology.

Nuclear Power

These are, quite frankly, hideously expensive and complicated to set up. Once they are up and running, however, the modern facilities are safe and efficient. The main drawback is disposing of the nuclear waste and the fact that they have to be situated away from any major settlements due to the strict regulations around radioactivity contamination risks.

They generate power continuously and can be adjusted to produce varying amounts depending on demand. This makes them an attractive option for major grid networks.

Wind Power

The very large size of the individual turbines makes them expensive to build and install. They also require large areas of land or sea. Off shore wind farms have similar problems to solar towers in that the electricity generated needs to be transmitted over long distances to be transferred into the grid. This is less of a problem for onshore facilities, and the ground they occupy can be used for other purposes, most notably agriculture.

The power supply is variable and, as each turbine requires power to keep the various lubrication and adjustment equipment operating, there is some debate about their overall efficiency. Some research seems to indicate that the nett power production is much lower than generally reported, although this is hotly disputed. Another possible disadvantage is that they have a limited lifespan (again there is a lot of debate around the actual figures) and so will need to be replaced at regular intervals. The latest figures indicate a lifespan of around 25 years, with a gradual decline in efficiency that can be mitigated by replacing worn out or damaged parts. Wind turbines installed in the early 1990's currently produce on average about 75% of their original output. This means that the amount of pollution created in constructing and maintaining the wind farms is unlikely to decrease and the costs will continue to be an important factor.

There are also concerns about the impact on the local environment based around the low resonance vibrations they produce in the ground and the number of local and migratory birds that fly into the turbines.

It is also apparent that they create turbulence and thus changes to the local wind patterns behind them. This has been measured in associated local temperature and weather pattern changes. If you subscribe to the 'Butterfly Effect' theory then the large scale of these farms has to have an effect on the global weather patterns which will only increase as more are built.

One other problem is that this is an industry with huge amounts of investment and research. Some of the advances (bladeless technologies being a prime example) will make the current turbine designs obsolete before they reach the end of their useful lifespan. This poses the question of whether to hold back the new technologies until the current turbines need to be replaced. The impact this will have on the companies that manufacture and install the equipment also has to be considered, especially when you factor in the huge subsidies currently paid by governments to support the industry.

<u>Hydro-electric</u>

Where the landscape and local environment are suitable, this is an obvious choice. Constructing dams is quite expensive but this is an ancient technology and very well understood. Once constructed they are reliable and relatively cheap to maintain.

The impact on the local environment can be severe if large reservoirs are required and changing the flow of major rivers can adversely affect the environment for hundreds of miles downstream.

Overall, if environmental impacts are kept to a minimum, this is a safe, reliable and relatively cheap way of manufacturing electricity on a medium to large scale.

Geothermal

In countries where it is readily available this is a cheap and reliable source of energy. As well as using it to generate electricity, it can be used for heating and, of course, natural hot springs for relaxing, bathing and cleansing.

Tidal

Still in its infancy, tidal energy has plenty of potential but is expensive to set up. The world's first large scale tidal stream farm (that's what they're being called at the moment) became operational in the Pentland Firth just outside Inverness in the Scottish Highlands during 2016. Called MeyGen, when fully completed it is expected to supply enough electricity to power 175,000 homes. For a detailed analysis click here.

Whilst tidal energy is predictable and easier to harness than wind power, it uses a similar technology of turbines. It is very expensive to install but after that the cost of generating electricity is very low. At the moment it is limited to near-shore locations and there are concerns about the impact on the local environment.

Wave

This is a relatively simple and cost effective way of generating electricity. It is ideal for near shore installations and has a minimal impact on the marine environment. In fact, some research shows that a 'wave farm' could create a more stable coastal habitat and reduce coastal erosion.

Solar Arrays

Solar cell efficiency is increasing all the time, whilst the size and cost is reducing at a similar rate. For large scale use it requires a lot of land, but as with wind farms, the land can still be used for farming and livestock.

Solar arrays are relatively inexpensive to set up and have minimal running costs. As with all forms of solar energy, they only generate electricity during the day.

14 Small scale energy production (for local and individual use)

<u>Fuel cells</u>

For vehicles, this is the ideal power source to replace diesel and petrol internal combustion engines. There is a growing interest in fuel cells globally and they are becoming cheaper and more eficient all the time. For them to really become mainstream, all that is required is a fuel network, and this is starting to be addressed.

There are a few major advantages that FCEVs have over electric vehicles. They currently have a greater range and only take five minutes to refuel, whereas the best of the EVs still require around eight hours to fully recharge, and while this is reducing all the time, it will almost certainly be at least ten years before the recharging time is less than an hour. Advances in storage batteries is extending their range as well, but the electricity to charge them comes from the grid. As most countries do not have much spare capacity, the mass use of EVs will cause major problems without large scale investment to increase the grid capacity. How the electricity is generated directly affects how green the use of EVs can be.

FCEVs provide a very similar user experience to current vehicles in that you drive them until they need fuel and you then fill it up in a few minutes and continue on your way. They have the added advantage of being a mobile electricity generator.

Fuel cells can also be installed in houses and small buildings to supply electricity on demand. They are proving to be a cheap, reliable and clean source of electricity.

This is the most important renewable technology for the future and needs to be promoted and supported as much as possible.

Solar Panels

There has already been a lot of take up globally for individual houses and small buildings and as the technology is constantly advancing this should only increase. It is ideal for remote areas. A new start-up business in Kenya is offering a solar powered satellite TV system designed for people in remote rural locations that is really helping to improve the lives of people. http://www.bbc.co.uk/news/business-38680093

This is another important renewable technology that needs as much support as possible.

Biomass

This is a great way to provide electricity in a local community environment. It uses waste materials (and can be installed as part of a water purification process), provides useful by-products and is a clean, reliable and relatively cheap way of producing electricity on a low to medium scale.

Wind

This is expensive and unreliable. My daughter's school had one installed in the mid 2000's and all of the pupils were very disappointed when the gauge showing the amount of electricity produced rarely rose enough to power one 60 watt lightbulb. As far as I can tell, wind turbines are not generally considered suitable for small scale use, although some modern building designs incorporate an Archimedes screw type of arrangement to capture wind at the edges of the building.

Geothermal

In areas where it is naturally available, this is an ideal source of heat and power for individual to medium scale use and is cheap and reliable.

Tidal

This is expensive to set up and maintain and can only generate electricity at certain times of day. It is not suitable for individual or small scale power supply.

Wave

This appears to be a promising method of producing electricity for seaside towns and communities and once set up should be cheap and reliable. It could also improve the local marine environment.

Hydroelectric

As with wave and geothermal sources, this is a reliable way to generate electricity on a small to medium scale where it is naturally available.

15 Combining different technologies

It is obvious to me that the best way forward with green and renewable energy is to combine them.

For grid networks more needs to be done to use each type where it is naturally available. Wind farms already receive huge amounts of investment. We need to commit more resources into developing the various ways of generating power from the oceans, seas, rivers and waterways, particularly wave and tidal power. By combining all of the natural resources available, increasing the use of biomass generation and investing in new technologies I am convinced that most countries could do away with the need for coal, nuclear and gas powered generators within a relatively short period (between 25 and 50 years, depending on the country and the amount of external investment). By encouraging the take up of small scale and individual power generation the demands on the grid would be reduced as well. There is also a method called combined heat and power (CHP), or cogeneration. It basically involves using the excess heat to supply hot water and increase the efficiency of the generating process. The explain that stuf f website has a good basic description.

For transport and energy self-sufficient housing and buildings there are a few interesting options. The one that I feel is an obvious pairing is solar and hydrogen. Solar panels generate electricity which can be used directly and also generate hydrogen fuel by electrolysis which is used in fuel cells to provide electricity on demand. There is a lot of research and development going into this and early adopter systems are already available. The Japanese ENE-FARM project is the most successful so far.

Printed in Great Britain
by Amazon

35046641R00066